Radio–Electronics®
Guide to
Computer
Circuits

Radio-Electronics®

Guide to

Computer
Circuits

Editors of
Radio-Electronics®

TAB BOOKS Inc.

Blue Ridge Summit, PA

FIRST EDITION

FIRST PRINTING

Copyright © 1988 by TAB BOOKS Inc.

Printed in the United States of America

Library of Congress Cataloging in Publication Data

Radio-electronics guide to computer circuits / by editors of Radio-electronics.
    p. cm.
   Includes index.
   ISBN 0-8306-0333-6 ISBN 0-8306-9333-5 (pbk.)
    1. Electronic digital computers—Circuits. I. Radio-electronics.
II. Title: Guide to computer circuits.
TK7888.4.R33 1988
621.395—dc19   88-11795
                                              CIP

Questions regarding the content of this book should be addressed to:

   Reader Inquiry Branch
   TAB BOOKS Inc.
   Blue Ridge Summit, PA 17294-0214

Contents

Preface

THIS BOOK CONSISTS OF ARTICLES FROM THE "DRAWING Board," "Designer's Notebook," and the "New Ideas" sections of the *Radio Electronics* magazine from the February 1984 to August 1987 period. All of the material deals with microprocessors and related hardware and software on the hobbyist level.

We hope the information we have accumulated and the projects presented here will prove to be both useful and enjoyable to you.

Section 1: LOGIC

THIS SECTION PROVIDES SOME THOUGHT-PROVOKING POSSI-bilities for the experimenter using logic gates, and even making your own logic probe.

SINGLE-GATE CIRCUITS

Whenever most of us think about circuit-design shortcuts or tricks to make life easier, it usually involves taking a handful of familiar circuit elements and using them in a way *not* mentioned in the data books. Plenty of brainwork goes into saving time and energy and, of course, component cost. In general, the slicker the trick, the simpler the design and the greater the savings. We're going to look at the simplest design you can possibly have—one gate!

For the purpose of this discussion we'll be looking at an exclusive-or (XOR) gate. You can use the 4070 CMOS version or, if you're into TTL design, you can pick any of the 7486 family. The XOR gate is a really useful device when you're thinking about a one-gate design. But, just how much can you do with a single gate? Well, let's see.

Exclusive-or Circuits

Figure 1-1A shows the symbol for the XOR gate along with its truth table. The truth table shows that its output is low whenever both inputs are the same, and high if the inputs are different. (That's an important characteristic, as we shall soon see). The most immediate use for that truth table is to build the world's cheapest phase detector. All we have to do is route the two signals in question to the inputs of the gate and hang an LED on the output. Two possible layouts are shown in Figs. 1-1B and 1-1C. The Fig. 1-1B circuit shows an XOR gate with its out being fed to an LED and resistor in series.

The LED's cathode is tied to ground through the resistor. When the two inputs are equal (both high or both low), the output of the gate is low. On the other hand, when the inputs are out of phase (one high and one low), the gate outputs a high. That forward-biases the LED, thus causing it to light. Now, if we turn LED around and connect its cathode to +V, as shown in Fig. 1-1C, it will light when the inputs are in phase. What could be simpler?

Another possibility is shown in Fig. 1-1D. Here we see that if we replace LED 1 with a tri-color LED and tie it to a point halfway up the supply rail, it will be one color when the inputs are in phase and another color when they're not. Let's see why that happens. To understand how the circuit operates, we must first look into the matter of how a tri-color LED works.

The tri-color LED can be thought of as two LED's connected anode to cathode in parallel. (It's not quite that simple, but, for discussion's sake, we'll use that illustration.) Anyway, when the voltage is negative, one LED will be forward-biased and will therefore light (let's say red). But, when the voltage is positive (or reversed) the other LED will light—this time green. The third color (yellow) lights when an ac voltage is applied, but we won't get into that this time. Now, let's get back to our circuit.

Let's say that the two inputs to our gate are in phase (both high). That drives the gate output low; that low is

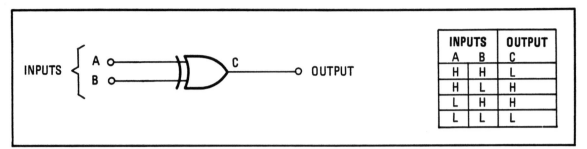

Fig. 1-1A.

INPUTS		OUTPUT
A	B	C
H	H	L
H	L	H
L	H	H
L	L	L

Fig. 1-1B.

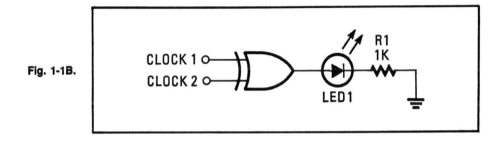

Fig. 1-1C.

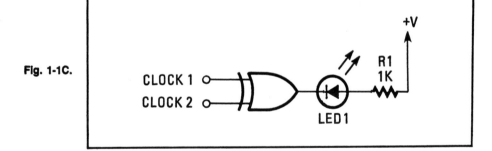

Fig. 1-1D.

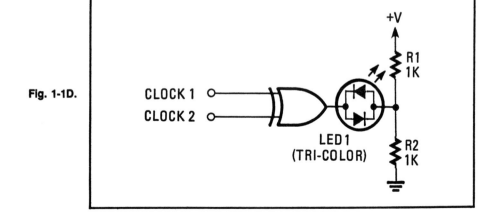

then applied to the tri-color LED, causing one color to light (let's say red). But why not both? Remember, only one LED is forward-biased at a time, therefore only one will light—it's just that simple. Now, we've all built "cheapo" oscillators using a pair of inverters; but, as you will see, the XOR lets us cut the gate count in half!

Figure 1-1E shows a clock circuit that we can build using just one gate and a resistor. Although its operation is reliable, it is *not* as stable as an oscillator built from two inverters. However, if all you need is a clock, try that circuit.

So that you can understand why it works, let's see what is actually going on in that circuit. First, let's assume that the output of the circuit in Fig. 1-1E is high. Since the B input is tracking the output, it will be high as well. If we apply a high to input A (making both inputs high), the output will go low. That makes input B low, thus driving the output high again, and the whole cycle starts all over.

What you can expect to get from that circuit will depend on the level of voltage (+ V) and the resistor value you use. If you're using a CMOS gate you will find that the output swing is less than you would get with a more traditional design. The output will only have an amplitude of about 80 percent of the supply. The frequency you get will depend on the supply because you have a resistor in line and a certain amount of time has to go by before input B "sees" enough voltage to make the gate change states.

Obviously the value of the resistor is going to come into play as well. Experiment with different values, but make sure you stay above 10,000 ohms or so. If you use a supply of about 7 volts (a 9-volt battery) and the resistor

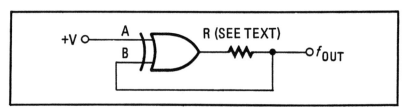

Fig. 1-1E.

value is around 50,000 ohms, you should be able to get about 5 MHz out of the gate.

The actual frequency is also somewhat dependent on the IC itself. The propagation delay of the gate (the time it takes to change state) is about 100 nanoseconds at 7 volts; which translates, theoretically speaking, into a maximum frequency of 10 MHz. The delay caused by the resistor will cut that amount by about half, and individual gates behave differently. Play with the circuit and see what you come up with. You will find, however, that the supply voltage and not the individual gate, is the most important variable.

There are many other useful things you can do with only one gate. The XOR is a versatile gate and there are lots of other handy-dandy things you can do with it. But don't overlook the rest of the logic gates.

LOGIC-FAMILY TRANSLATION

Everybody has his favorite logic family. Some like the familiarity of TTL and have never given CMOS a chance since the bad days of the CMOS "A" series devices. On the other hand, some like CMOS and think that anyone hung up on TTL is from the stone age. DTL and RTL users are primarily history.

The truth of the matter is that both TTL and CMOS are going to be around for a while because each has advantages and disadvantages. If you look at enough schematics, you'll see that many circuit designers routinely mix both logic families in the same electronics package.

There are several considerations to keep in mind if you want to do the same thing in your own designs. Mixing logic families requires that you pay attention to the voltage at which they change state. TTL parts have much stricter requirements than CMOS. A TTL low state has a maximum voltage of about 0.8, and a TTL high state has a minimum voltage of 2.4. CMOS, on the other hand, is much more flexible. A low is usually defined as less than half the supply voltage, and a high is more than half the supply voltage.

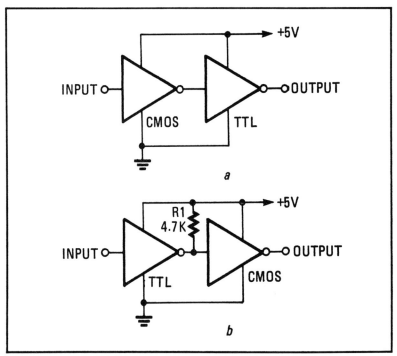

Fig. 1-2.

If you're working with a five-volt-only circuit, mixing TTL and CMOS is simple. As you can see in Fig. 1-2A, driving a single TTL input with a CMOS output requires nothing more than connecting the two parts together. Going from TTL to CMOS, however, requires a bit more thought. Assuming a five-volt supply, the TTL high output can be as low as 2.4 volts. That's slightly below the point at which the CMOS input will change state, so there's no guarantee that the circuit will work correctly. The solution is to add a pull-up resistor of about 4.7K, as shown in Fig. 1-2B. The exact value of the resistor depends on the type of TTL you're using (74, 74S, 74LS, etc.), but a value of 4.7K at least will get you in the ballpark.

DIFFERENT SUPPLY VOLTAGES

Things get even more tricky if the CMOS and TTL halves of your circuit are powered by different voltages. Two readily available CMOS buffers (the 4049 and the 4050) can translate the higher voltage CMOS output into

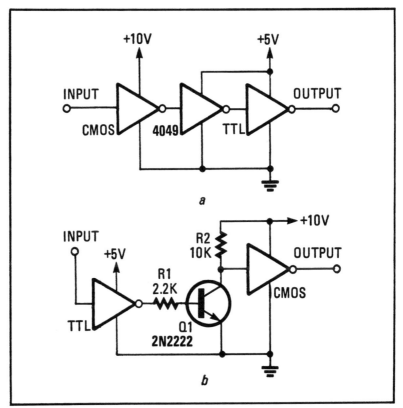

Fig. 1-3.

something the TTL input can use. A sample circuit is shown in Fig. 1-3A. To make the translation without inverting the signal, use a 4050.

Going from TTL at 5 volts to CMOS at, say, 10 volts, requires some voltage translation. We can't always do it the way we did in Fig. 1-2B because the TTL output must be isolated from the higher CMOS voltage.

There are many schemes to get the job done, but an easy one is shown in Fig. 1-3B. A small-signal NPN transistor is used as a buffering switch between the TTL and the CMOS parts, but keep in mind that the transistor will invert the signal from the TTL output. You can re-invert the signal by using another transistor or a spare CMOS gate.

FANOUT

Before we leave the subject of logic-family translation,

we must talk about fanout. If you're a regular CMOS user, you're probably used to ignoring fanout limits altogether. The reason is that the input impedance of a typical CMOS part is so high that you can drive as many inputs as you want with a single output. The same is true when driving CMOS with TTL: A typical TTL output has more than enough current-capacity to drive any number of CMOS inputs. Going the other way, however, is a bit of a problem.

The reason is that most CMOS outputs simply can't deliver much current into a low-impedance TTL input. The number of TTL inputs you can drive with a CMOS output depends on the specific TTL part you're using. As a general rule you can drive more LS inputs than regular or S inputs, but it's usually better to be safe than sorry. So don't drive more than two inputs, regardless of type. As a matter of fact, it's better not to drive more than one, and make it a 7404 or 74S04. You'll have no trouble whatsoever driving the single input and then following the standard rules for TTL-to-TTL fanout.

If you anticipate designing many mixed-family logic circuits, work out each problem on a breadboard and standardize the design. By doing so, any time you're faced with the same problem, you'll have a debugged module you can drop in your circuit and solve the problem. And that will let you go on to more important things.

INVERTING LOGIC OSCILLATORS

One of the nicest things about digital circuits is that you can make an oscillator out of just about anything. Just look around your design and find a few spare parts (unused gates on the board), connect them together and you've got an oscillator. While working with analog components requires some thought, digital stuff is just lying there, begging for the chance to squirt out squarewaves. But that kind of convenience tends to make you sloppy.

Because most gate-type oscillators are essentially trouble free, you can easily get into the habit of thinking that they all are—but they're not! Everybody is familiar

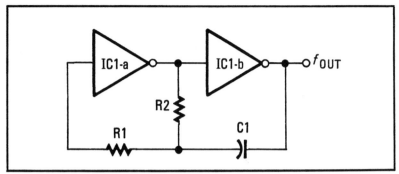

Fig. 1-4.

with (and has used) the oscillator arrangement shown in Fig. 1-4. (We've shown it with inverters, but any type of simple inverting logic will fill the bill.)

Oscillator Circuits

The circuit in Fig. 1-4 is simple to put together, forgiving of part values, and relatively stable for a given supply voltage. However, there is one problem associated with it—it won't always oscillate!

Like a good many of you, I've relied on that circuit whenever I needed a simple clock generator. More convenient ones, with fewer parts can be built with Schmitt triggers; however, not every circuit uses Schmitt triggers.

Imagine my surprise, after having figured out the component values for an oscillator I was building to get the clock frequency I wanted, and found that when I plugged the parts into the board, nothing happened. There I was, the victim of my own sloppiness.

The reason that the oscillator in Fig. 1-4 won't always work can be understood by taking the part values to the extremes—decreasing component values—and seeing what happens to the circuit. That kind of experimentation can come in handy when it comes to simplifying any circuit.

If we keep on reducing the value of capacitor C1 and let it go to zero, we're going to wind up with the circuit shown in Fig. 1-5. There we see that IC1-b is no longer a part of the circuit, and it doesn't take much analysis to see that the circuit won't oscillate. What that tells us

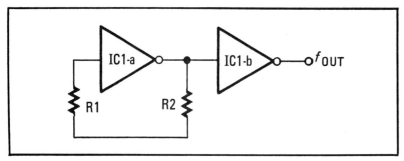

Fig. 1-5.

is that there are limits to the allowable value of the capacitor.

What those limits are will depend on several things; the supply voltage, load, component values, and a whole bunch of other stuff. In other words, what had been a really handy, no-thought type of circuit has turned into one that requires some consideration before we can use it.

The problem here is that the schematic in Fig. 1-4 is not an inherently astable circuit. That can be seen by looking at Fig. 1-5 and comparing it to Fig. 1-4. Remember, the capacitor forces the circuit to oscillate and if it's value is not large enough (or there is none at all), the circuit will just sit there and do absolutely nothing.

What we need is a trouble-free oscillator that is inherently astable. Figure 1-6 is the type of circuit that we're looking for. As stated before, you can do a lot better and greatly simplify things by using Schmitt triggers. For

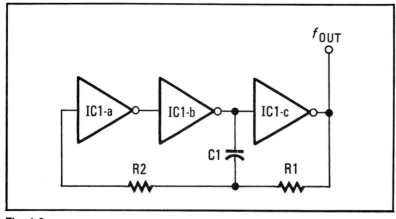

Fig. 1-6.

all those other times, however, the circuit shown in Fig. 1-6 is just what the doctor ordered.

The circuit is sure-starting and trouble-free—it will oscillate over a much wider range than an oscillator made with just two inverters (like the one in Fig. 1-4). The formula for determining the output frequency is admittedly a bit complex, but several assumptions can greatly simplify things. Since it's not the kind of circuit that you would use if you need good stability or heavy-duty precision, the following approximations are more than adequate:

- If R1 is close to R2, then $f = .56/RC$, where R is the average of R1 and R2.
- If R1 is much larger than R2, then $f = .46/R1C$.
- If R1 is much smaller than R2, then $f = .722/R1C$.

The output will be a squarewave with a duty-cycle that's pretty close to 50/50. That only happens with CMOS inverters because the switching point is the threshold of the inverters and (for CMOS) that's halfway up the supply rail. That switching characteristic also makes the circuit almost immune to power-supply spikes and other nasties.

The output frequency of the circuit is a function of the propagation delay through the gates. That means that the output stability will degrade as the frequency increases. The propagation delay is a constant and the lower the frequency, the smaller it (the delay) will be relative to each output pulse.

A VERSATILE, LOW-COST LOGIC PROBE

The low-cost logic probe presented here is a must for anyone who experiments with digital circuits and whose budget can't tolerate a $35.00 logic probe in a fancy case. This circuit uses popular components, provides utility that rivals that of commercial units and, best of all, costs as little as $6.00 to build. The complete circuit is shown in Fig. 1-7A.

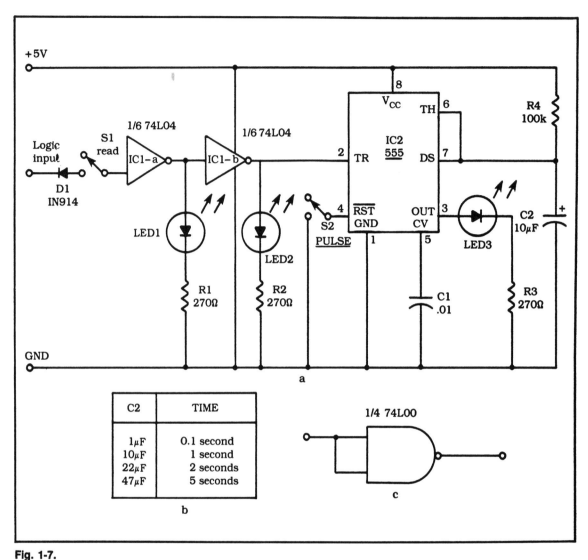

Fig. 1-7.

How It Works

Diode D1 is included for protection against reversed-polarity inputs. A logic-low input causes LED1 to light, and a logic-high input causes LED2 to light. The 555 acts as a pulse catcher; when PULSE switch S2 is open, LED3 lights up for about one second each time a pulse is detected. Resistor R4 and capacitor C2 determine the "on" time of LED3. To change that time, figure that for each 10 µF of capacitance, the LED will light for about

1 second. The table shown in Fig. 1-7B gives "on" times for several values of C2. Just remember that you don't want LED3 to stay on too long, or you might miss pulses.

Construction is not critical. If you wish you can wire the circuit on a piece of perfboard using either point-to-point or wire-wrap techniques.

You may want to use different colored LED's for LED1, LED2, and LED3—say green, red, and yellow. The green LED will indicate a logic low, the red LED a logic high, and the yellow LED a pulse. If you don't have a 74L04 handy, you can use a 74L00 as an inverter by tying both inputs from one gate together, as shown in Fig. 1-7C.

HOW TO USE IT

Connect-the +5 VOLT and GROUND terminals to the corresponding points in the circuit under test. Then attach the LOGIC INPUT terminal to the point you wish to monitor via a probe (such as a spare VOM probe) and close READ switch S1. Either LED1 or LED2 will light to indicate the state of that point. Switch S2, PULSE, should be open to use the pulse-catcher; closing it sends the 555 into a reset state, which forces the output low and turns off LED3.

The circuit was designed to work with TTL signals. It will probably work with CMOS, but it may load the circuit under test. Also, the 74L04 will only work with a 5-volt circuit.

Section 2: DESIGNING CONSIDERATIONS

CIRCUIT CONSTRUCTION IS RELATIVELY EASY, AND IT IS A skill that improves with experience. Designing microprocessor-based circuits requires considerable forethought to develop the desired, working project. This section presents some of the most important considerations for microprocessor circuits in general, and memory IC's and dynamic RAM's in particular.

DESIGNING MICROPROCESSOR-BASED CIRCUITS

In the past, we've spent plenty of time talking about gates, latches, flip-flops and counters. After all, anyone interested in circuit design needs a clear understanding of what those elements are, how they work, and how they can be used. Although logic families have changed—DLT having given way to RTL, and RTL to TTL and CMOS technologies—the basic design approach has not. Flow charts, block diagrams; and other paper work are all still necessary to obtain a final product.

Circuit design should begin with basic building blocks. But as technology advances, what once was an exotic part becomes so common that we begin to think of it as a basic element. And that's certainly true of the microprocessor.

Many people think that microprocessors are computers. Well, they're not. Computers are one application of microprocessors, but not the only one. Microprocessors are IC's that accept instructions, move data from place to place, and perform logical operations.

We'll look at microprocessors to see how they can be used to lower power requirements, and cut down the parts count and board size of typical circuits. What's more, you'll see how one basic circuit can be made to handle a multitude of jobs.

Microprocessors can control various elements of a circuit, but something has to tell them what to do and when. That means you'll finally have to come to terms with the great "god," software.

UNDERSTANDING MICROPROCESSORS

If you had to pinpoint the basic difference between a gates-only circuit and a microprocessor-based one, it would probably be that the former can do only the specific job it's designed to do, while the latter can do a number of different things, as long as it's properly told what to do. Everything depends on the set of instructions (software) fed to the microprocessor. But for now, let's examine the internal structure of the microprocessor to see what's inside and how it works. Once we have a clear understanding of that, we can start telling it what to do.

Basically, there are two types of microprocessors: top-down and bottom-up. The difference has as much to do with how they handle memory as with their internal organization.

Microprocessors spend a lot of time moving and manipulating data, and they need a place to store the interim and resulting data. The way they handle that task marks another basic difference between the two types of microprocessors. The bottom-up type has internal registers that can be used for data storage, "housekeeping," counters, and so on. The top-down type uses external memory for the same purpose.

Figure 2-1 should give you a better idea of what I mean. The Z80 (Fig.2-1A) and 6502 (Fig. 2-1B) are perfect examples, respectively, of a bottom-up and a top-down microprocessor or CPU (*Central Processing Unit*). The Z80 has a total of 14 general-purpose internal registers, while the 6502 has only two. Both have the other registers that all microprocessors need: the accumulator, the stack pointer, the flag register, and so on. We'll cover all of those eventually.

The number of registers doesn't necessarily make one microprocessor better than another; only different. However, that difference can make one better suited for a particular application than another. A CPU with many internal registers (bottom-up) can manipulate data between the registers very quickly. But they slow down when they have to access external memory.

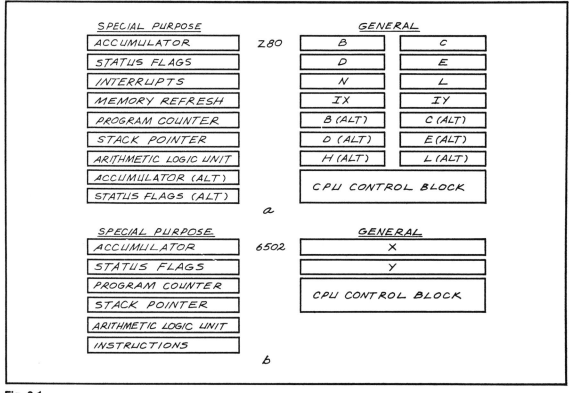

Fig. 2-1.

On the other hand, a top-down microprocessor like the 6502 uses external memory for almost everything it does, but it has a speedy way of accessing the bottom range of external memory. By contrast, all external memory appears the same way to bottom-up microprocessors (another topic for future discussion).

Microprocessors with many internal registers (like the Z80) can move and manipulate data from register to register very quickly, making number-crunching faster—a definite asset in applications doing a lot of arithmetic. But the 6502 is capable of doing BCD (*Binary Coded Decimal*) math. If BCD is used, the round-off errors that crop up in binary math (the normal way arithmetic computations are handled in that and other microprocessors) are avoided.

Finally, if you're doing a lot of I/O operations, the simpler bus interface requirements of the 6502 are worthy of serious consideration. In any case, when dealing with microprocessors, remember that anything you can do with one, you can also do with another, although maybe not as easily.

Since learning to use a CPU means putting in plenty of time, you should pick your microprocessor carefully. I've chosen to use the Z80 for discussion; it's cheap, available, powerful, and there's a wide range of support IC's available for it. To design microprocessor-based circuits you must first understand exactly what the microprocessor can do, and how it does it.

Figure 2-2 shows a block diagram of the internal structure of the Z80. As you study it, notice that it isn't really much different from the circuits we've designed in the past. In fact, it would be possible—although not really practical—to build a CPU from discrete logic IC's.

The Z80, like most other microprocessors is made up of five different parts: the instruction decoder, the CPU control block, the address and data bus controllers, the ALU (*Arithmetic Logic Unit*), and the storage registers. What separates a CPU from just a collection of discrete elements is the inclusion of the ALU and the instruction decoder.

The ALU is the workhorse of the CPU. That is where

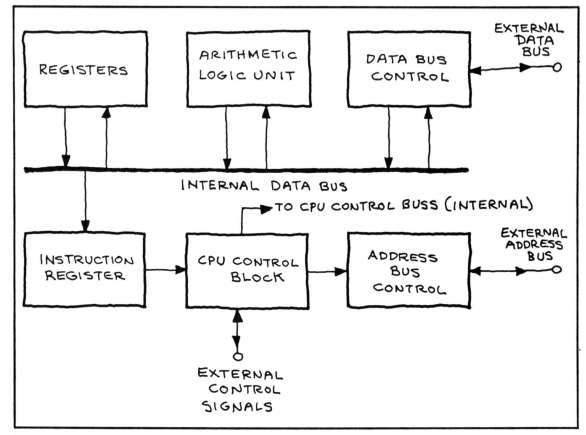

Fig. 2-2.

addition, subtraction, logical operations (AND, OR, XOR, NOT) and other operations occur. Precisely what goes on in the ALU depends upon another part of the CPU—the instruction decoder.

The instruction decoder is the part of the CPU that contains the instruction set (a preprogrammed series of routines that are performed when the CPU receives the appropriate command). The instruction decoder mediates between the ALU and external memory. It is the job of the instruction decoder to recognize a command, decode it, and issue the appropriate instructions to the ALU. The ALU acts accordingly and then waits for the next set of instructions. The series of commands that the instruction decoder receives, of course, is the program being run.

Translating low-level data manipulation into useful

work requires plenty of additional hardware and the right software. As with everything else we've done together, you're going to be doing a lot of work on paper before you ever look at a soldering iron. The first—and probably the most important—thing you have to do before we continue our discussion is to get a good book on the Z80 and start reading. Either of TAB's books "The Programming Guide to the Z80™ Chip" #1656, or "101 Projects for the Z80™" #1491 are fine selections by Phillip R. Robinson and Frank P. Tedeschi respectively. There's just no way to fit all the necessary information into this column.

Our next step will be to put together a bare-bones Z80 system and see what can be done with it. If you're new to microprocessors, I think you'll be amazed by its versatility.

DESIGNING WITH MEMORY IC'S

Everyone knows that there's a world of difference between theory and practice in electronics. As we've seen time and time again, what works perfectly well on paper tends to blow up perfectly well on the breadboard. I can't tell you how many times I've helplessly sat back and watched acres of silicon "real estate" go up in smoke at the speed of light!

One way to avoid blowing up expensive or even inexpensive components is to be really familiar with the eccentricities of the device. That applies to everything in your design and not only IC's. Switches, relays, batteries and even lowly resistors have operating peculiarities that can screw things up under what would seem to be the most ordinary of circumstances. Therefore, it is best to know a little something about a component before you begin using it.

The best way to learn about any electronic component is to pick up a few and do a little experimenting, or build a demonstration circuit. Nowhere is that more true than when designing memory-based circuits. Using a demonstration circuit lets you learn to safely use a particular memory, and see what requirements have to be kept in mind for its use in general.

Now, there's no single circuit you can design that will teach you everything about all types of memory. And even if we limit our discussion to RAM, we'll find that looking at one type won't teach us everything we need to know. (We've already seen that there's a big difference between the *static* and *dynamic* types.) So that you may become familiar with the fundamentals, let's start off with *static* RAM. When we're done, we'll see that only a few additions and changes have to be made to accommodate *dynamic* RAM.

STATIC RAM

For our discussion we'll be using the *5101* 256 × 4 RAM. There are several advantages to using that IC: It's cheap, (under $3 mail-order), widely available, CMOS, and features a low-power data retention mode so a battery can be used to back up stored data.

Several manufacturers make the 5101 and although there are minor differences between them, any one you can get your hands on will be fine for our purposes. Table 2-1 is a listing of several pin-for-pin equivalents of the 5101. The variations in the IC usually have to do with things like maximum operating-voltage, access time, and the like. If we keep the supply at 5 volts and are willing to live with a 450-nanosecond access time, we can forget about the differences altogether.

Figure 2-3 shows the pinout of the 5101. A block diagram of the IC's innards is shown in Fig. 2-4, but it's no substitute for a data sheet. The timing diagrams and such that are found on data sheets are *absolutely invaluable* when you're using memory IC's. You can

TABLE 2-1

AMI—S5101 (any suffix)	NEC—5101
HARRIS—6561	RCA—MWS5101 or CDP1822
HITACHI—435101	(any suffix)
INTEL—5101	SSS—5101
NATIONAL—74C920 or NMC6551	SYNERTEX—5101
MOTOROLA—145101	TOSHIBA—5101

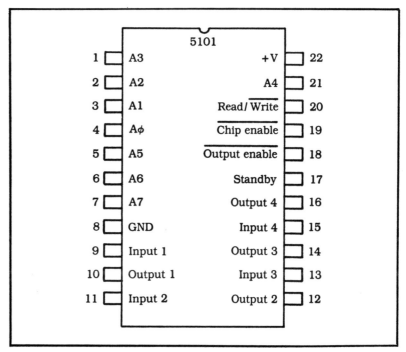

Fig. 2-3.

build a demonstration circuit without them, but you'll learn a lot more if you have them in front of you while you work. (Think of it as a poor man's substitute for an oscilloscope.)

The first step in designing the demonstration circuit or any other circuit, for that matter, is to have a perfectly clear idea in your mind of exactly what you want the circuit to do. That means we first must list all design criteria, and then draw a block diagram of the circuit. Once that's done, we can actually begin the breadboarding. The design criteria for our circuit are:

- Keyboard entry of data and address
- Switch control of read and write
- Random read and write operations
- Display of address, data in, and data out
- Automatic keyboard sequencing of address and data
- Keyboard control of all memory functions and modes

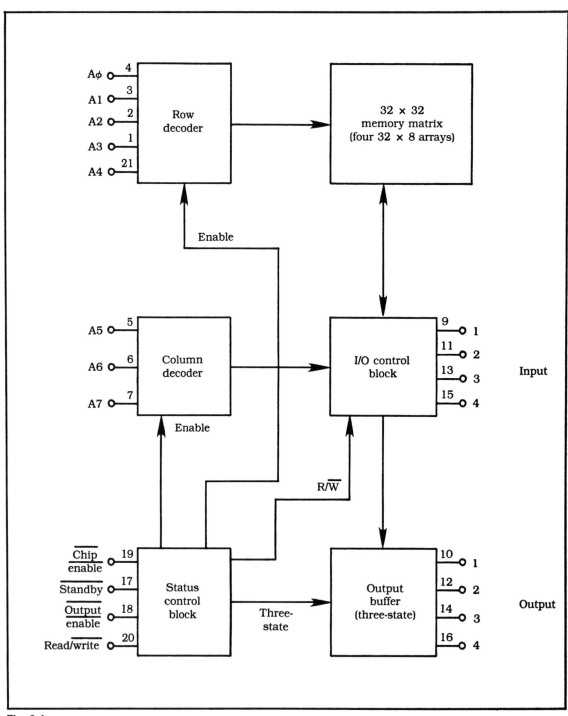

Fig. 2-4.

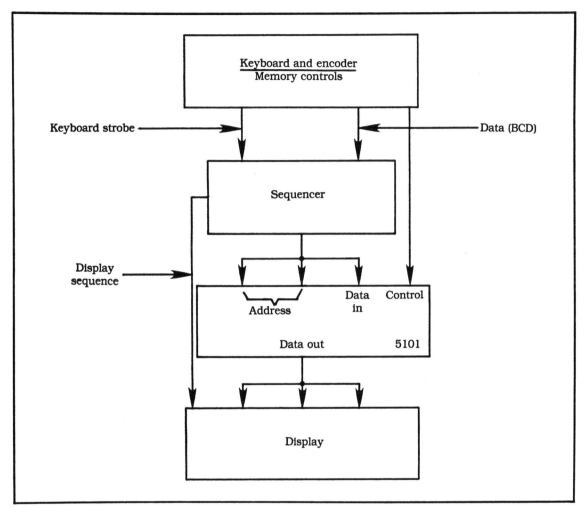

Fig. 2-5.

A block diagram of a circuit that meets those requirements is shown in Fig. 2-5

DESIGNING WITH DYNAMIC RAM'S

The more that you mess around with memory, the more uses you find for it. And the more uses you find, the more memory you want. That kind of reasoning led to the development of the *D*ynamic RAM (DRAM). Computers, for example, are memory-hungry machines, and every IC manufacturer has jumped into the race to develop a memory that packs more storage in less space.

At first glance, DRAM seems to be the answer to everybody's memory problems. The cost per bit of storage is much lower than that of static RAM, and manufacturers are constantly finding new ways to stuff more storage space into a standard package.

In no time at all, DRAM went from 16K to 256K per package. While the initial cost per unit was high, prices have dropped dramatically. For instance, the price of a 4164, 64K × 1 DRAM went from $50 to about $5 in less than 5 years!

With all obvious advantages of DRAM—plenty of storage, small packages, all at a reasonable price—why doesn't everyone use them? The answer is that they're a pain in the neck to use. Unless mountains of memory is an absolute necessity, you can save yourself plenty of brain damage by sticking to the reliable static RAM.

USING DYNAMIC RAM

There are two main hassles that must be dealt with to use DRAM's: data refresh and address multiplexing. The former is a consequence of the way data is stored, and the latter is a result of practical considerations.

When you start talking about packing up to 256K of storage (for now) in a single IC, you're rapidly going to run out of available pins. To illustrate, take a look at a 4164 and count the number of pins needed to make it work.

Since 4164 is organized in an 8K by 8K matrix, sixteen address lines are needed (8 rows and 8 columns) to access any particular bit in the matrix. Add to that pins for the I/O, power, ground, and a read/write control and we wind up needing 21 pins for a bare-bones memory.

Obviously, more pins are needed as storage capacity is increased. IC designers came up with a way to cut the pin count by using address multiplexing. That means that the internal row and column decoders are connected to the IC's address pins. The decoders are really latches that are controlled by the *Row Address Strobe* (RAS) and *Column Address Strobe* (CAS) pins on the IC.

That may sound complicated, but if you look at Fig.

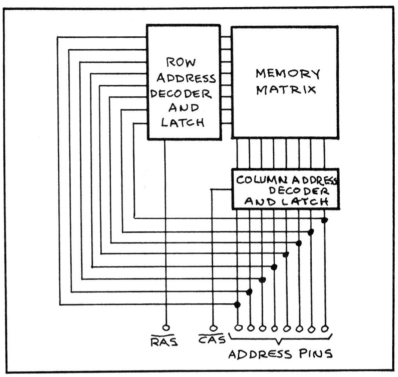

Fig. 2-6.

2-6, you'll have a much clearer understanding. Although address multiplexing makes things theoretically simple, it creates nightmares from a practical point of view because of the very strict timing requirements. Things are further complicated by the second DRAM hassle—memory refresh.

DRAM uses tiny capacitors as memory-storage elements. But the charge on any one cell leaks quickly. Therefore, each cell must be refreshed at least once every two milliseconds.

There are three basic approaches to successfully using DRAM—gates only, dedicated IC's, and microprocessors. The first two approaches are similar. If you use only gates to take care of the basic RAM requirements, the block diagram of your circuit will be similar to Fig. 2-7. Notice that the system-address bus has been split into separate row and column lines going to the memory matrix.

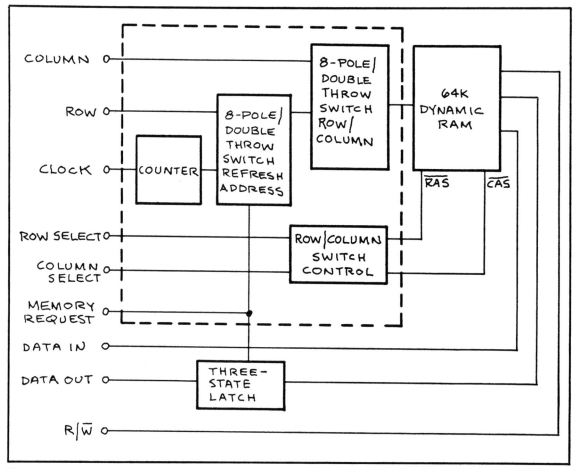

Fig. 2-7.

Most modern DRAM's are set up so that when a cell is accessed in a particular row, the entire row of cells is automatically refreshed. If your circuit accesses each row often enough to meet the refresh requirements, then you don't have to worry about that problem. That kind of "hidden" refresh is the simplest solution to the whole problem.

But, not all circuits meet those requirements so the problem of refresh has to be (excuse the pun) addressed directly. In Fig. 2-7, the row portion of the address bus goes through an 8-pole, double-throw switch that's controlled by a MEMORY REQUEST line. When that line is inactive, RAS (ROW ADDRESS SELECT) is enabled, read is selected, and the memory-address pins are connected to the output of the counter by the refresh switcher.

That counter cycles over and over at a rate fast enough to refresh the memory. When the memory is accessed, the correct address is put on the address bus; the refresh switcher disconnects the counter, and feeds the row information to the row/column switcher. The row and column data is clocked into the memory by the system logic that controls the row/column select, and the appropriate data is stored in the output data latch. As soon as that happens, the memory-request line shifts back to the refresh setup.

If things are done too slowly, too quickly, or out of logical sequence, you'll probably lose your data and you're guaranteed to lose your temper. And that brings us to an unwritten law that should be immediately jotted down: You can't design with DRAM without using a data sheet.

The complexity of using DRAM has brought about a series of LSI IC's designed to take care of the whole business. Among those IC's are the 3200 series from Motorola and Intel, which contain all the circuitry needed to handle the refresh and address multiplexing requirements of mainstream DRAM's.

At a cost of under $10, they can go a long way toward simplifying your memory-support circuitry. You should remember, however, that it's possible to do the whole job with a handful of logic IC's as well. For a first-time designer or experimenter, it's better to use the gates-only approach. It's a good exercise in digital design.

Most DRAM's generate valid data as soon as the addressing is completed, but lack the chip-select controls found in static RAM, As a result, three-state latches or some other type of arrangement are always necessary to manage the data from the memory. That's particularly true if data has to flow two ways on the system data bus.

Computers are always loaded with bidirectional buffers and drivers since data is constantly going to and from the memory. The last method for massaging DRAM brings us to the topic that we'll cover later—microprocessors. Instead of using tons of gates or dedicated IC's, the whole problem can be handled with a microprocessor and a little software.

In fact, some microprocessors, like the Z80, have built-in routines for refreshing DRAM. People constantly forget that computers are *only* one special application for microprocessors. We'll see how they can be used to control RAM, keyboards, power supplies, and even the light on the back porch.

Section 3: POWER CONSIDERATIONS

Two very important aspects of microprocessor-based circuitry are power related. If you are working with CMOS circuits you will most likely want to build the battery backup in this section. On the other hand, if you are using 60 Hz circuitry you will definitely want to eliminate as much rfi and ripple as possible. We've included the capacitance multiplier to cure this frustrating condition.

A BATTERY BACKUP FOR CMOS-BASED CIRCUITS

One of the biggest advantages of CMOS-based circuit design is the ability to run everything off batteries. Not only does that make the circuit completely portable, but it simplifies the overall design process as well. Powering a device from a wall socket means that you have to use transformers and rectifiers. It also means that you have to deal with ripple, regulation, and a lot of other stuff that has nothing to do with the circuit you're trying to build.

Of course, there are two sides to every story. Batteries simplify a lot of problems, but they also have one big one of their own—they go dead. And if power is drawn by a circuit to retain memory, those batteries will fail a lot sooner.

Memories like the 5101, 6116, 6264, and the other members of the CMOS low-power series require only about 10 μA at 2 volts to retain their contents. That makes it possible to use a battery backup with those devices.

BATTERY BACKUP CIRCUIT

If a battery backup is to be of any use, you need a circuit that will automatically switch from the main supply to the battery backup with an absolute minimum of glitching. That's the purpose of the circuit shown in Fig. 3-1. Designed for use with rechargeable Ni-Cd units, it charges the batteries whenever power is applied to the +V terminal, and supplies power from B1 when power is absent from that terminal. The circuit is easily modified for use with non-rechargeable batteries.

The first thing you should notice about the circuit is its simplicity. The circuit's operation is straightforward. When power is supplied to +V, D1 conducts and, since D2 is reverse-biased, current flows into the batteries through current limiter R1. When the power is removed from +V, D2 is forward-biased and current flows from the battery to the output and on to the low-power voltage input of the CMOS device. Since D1 is reverse-biased at that time, no current can leak out via the +V terminal to the main part of the circuit. Capacitor C1 is included to filter out any glitches that may pop up during the

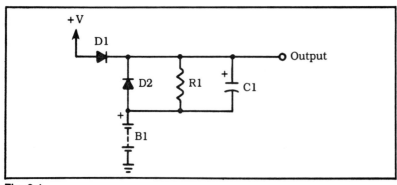

Fig. 3-1.

change-over from main power to battery backup, or when you replace the battery.

COMPONENT SELECTION

Diode D2 can be a 1N914 unit since only small amounts of current will ever flow through it. Choosing a unit for D2 presents more of a problem; its selection depends on 'how much current is expected to flow through that diode. Chances are, if you're powering a CMOS IC, that the operating current is so low that you can use a 1N914 there as well, It is a simple matter to measure the current needs of the device to be powered; that should be done before making a decision about which diode to use for D2.

Resistor R1 is the current limiter for the battery. Its value will depend on the battery's charging current and the voltage that's available from +V. The value can be found from:

$$R1 = (+V - 0.6 - V_B) \div I_C$$

where +V is the voltage available at the +V terminal, 0.6 is the voltage drop across diode D1, V_B is the nominal voltage of the battery, and I_C is the charge current required by the battery. For I_C use the battery's 14-hour charge rate. The value of I_C might be different for batteries from different manufacturers. The value for the battery you will use may be marked on the battery itself. Otherwise it can be obtained from the battery's data sheet or from the manufacturer. You can modify the circuit for use with lithium or other non-rechargeable units by deleting R1.

STABILIZING CONTROL LINES

One precaution you should take when using the circuit is to make sure that the memory control lines are stable before switching from main power to backup. If the control lines are enabled during the switch over, you stand a good chance of generating a write pulse and scrambling the data. In most cases, it's possible to three-state the appropriate inputs on the IC, which will take care of the problem. Otherwise, extra circuitry can be added that will perform the same function.

A SIMPLE SOLUTION TO POWER-SUPPLY RIPPLE

One common problem that plagues everybody who plays around with electronics hardware is power-supply noise. How critical that problem is depends entirely on the sort of circuit you want to power. Some circuits will "laugh off" ripple as high as ten percent of the supply voltage, while others will go "belly up" if any ripple at all is present.

Of course, there are several different kinds of power-supply noise—ac ripple and rf are two. How you go about dealing with the problem depends on the kind of noise you have. With all due respect to Einstein and his *Unified Field* theory, curing rfi is a lot different than dealing with poor regulation.

Probably the most common cause of noise is poor regulation in the supply. The 60-Hz that surrounds us has a nasty habit of finding its way into the output stages of even the most carefully regulated supply. That means when you put that plug into the wall socket, you usually get problems along with power!

Reducing ripple is a matter of careful power-supply design—proper shielding, and a whole host of other things we've all dealt with a million times. And if we had to point a finger at the single most important component in the elimination of ripple, it would have to be the filter capacitor that sits right on the output of the power supply.

More noise problems have been cured by increasing the size of that capacitor than by any other single means that I can think of. Unfortunately, finding huge capacitors is a practical problem and fitting them on the board is often a physical problem. However, there is a better way!

This "brainsaver" can go a long way toward solving the problem of unacceptable amounts of ripple. It's a very simple capacitance multiplier that works along with and helps the filter capacitor you put on the back end of your supply. If you use it intelligently, you'll be amazed at how quiet (ripple free) the dc can be.

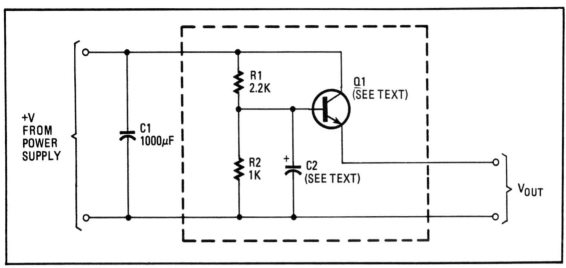

Fig. 3-2.

The operation of the circuit is virtually foolproof and it will easily stand up to a lot of experimenting. The basic design is flexible enough to operate with a wide range of component values. Figure 3-2 shows a schematic of the capacitance multiplier. The part values shown are a good starting point, and you should have no trouble getting the circuit to operate successfully.

How It Works

The transistor is set up as a high-gain amplifier that effectively amplifies C2, the capacitor connected to its base. Capacitor C1 is the regular filter capacitor you should have in the circuit to start off with. Since the circuit is in parallel with the filter capacitor, the net capacitance will be the sum of C1 and the "phony" capacitance of the multiplier.

The actual effective capacitance you can produce with that circuit depends on the value of C2 and the gain of transistor Q1. If you pick your values carefully for those two components, you can get a simulated capacitance of over 1 farad at the output and that's enough to quiet even the noisiest supply. (Yes, I said 1 farad, the equivalent of 1 million microfarads!)

As with any circuit, there are trade-offs—the thing that data books usually refer to euphemistically as *design considerations.* One glance at the circuit will show you that all the load current has to pass through the collector-emitter junction of the transistor. Therefore, you'd better make sure to pick a transistor for Q1 that can handle the current you're going to draw from the supply.

There's also going to be a voltage drop for the same reason, so make sure you feed the capacitance multiplier with a voltage that's about a volt or so higher than the value you want at the output. The effective capacitance of the circuit will be roughly the product of C2 and the gain of the transistor.

Since a good rule of thumb is that a transistor's gain decreases as its power handling capacity increases, you'll have to decide for yourself where the break-even point is for your application. If you really have a noise problem, and you want to handle large amounts of current, you might consider using a Darlington. Either the store-bought variety, or a home-made one put together from two transistors and some resistors will do the job. The key here is experimentation.

As with all the circuits that appear here, the schematic (Fig. 3-2) is only the starting point. What saves the day in one application will undoubtedly blow up in another. I'm sorry I can't give you exact values and part numbers for all the components, but the circuit's parts values are dictated by its use. The best advice I can give you is to breadboard the thing and start off with relatively small values. Use a 500-μF capacitor for C2, a 2N2222 for the transistor and see how the circuit operates.

Since you're dealing with a circuit that can emulate big capacitors, it pays to *exercise more than a bit of caution!* You'll be storing plenty of energy in a small place, and any circuit that can melt the tip of a screwdriver deserves to be treated with respect.

The voltage ratings of the capacitors should match up with the output of your supply—the higher the voltage rating of the capacitors the better. If you decide on the right components, the circuit can go a long way toward reducing hum in audio, and all the other nasties that ripple can produce. Just be careful; remember, you'll be dealing with increased amounts of energy.

Section 4: MEMORY CONSIDERATIONS

THIS SECTION APPROACHES THE ASPECTS OF CHOOSING which type of memory to experiment with, how it will be accessed, and how much available memory is "enough."

UNDERSTANDING MEMORY IC'S

There's no doubt that the electronic superstar of the 1980's is the computer. People are buying them like umbrellas in a rainstorm, whether they need them or not. In what has to be the classic case of consumer brainwashing, the public has been convinced that the list of life's basic necessities now includes a 64K memory. Well, it just ain't so!

There's a lot more to electronics than just computers. Died in the wool "hardware hackers" like you and me should look at computers the same way we look at any other piece of electronic equipment—as "hardwired databooks."

Understanding a few of the techniques used in putting those machines together can go a long way in solving problems that show up in our own designs. The nice part about dealing with computers on that level is that you don't have to buy one. All you really need is a good databook that describes computer circuitry and explains its operation.

Computers are heavily memory-dependent machines, and plenty of design time has gone into developing memory techniques that are as efficient as possible. Memory can make your life on the bench a lot

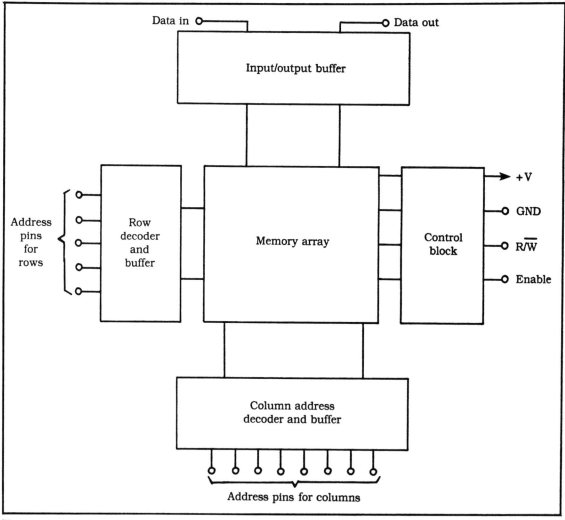

Fig. 4-1.

easier as well, so it's definitely worth the time to take a good look at memory devices.

Computers use both ROM, (*Read-Only Memory*) and RAM (*Random-Access Memory*). We'll start with the RAM since it's a lot more fun to play around with your own data. (We'll talk about ROM in a future discussion.)

RAM comes in two flavors—*static* and *dynamic*. The difference between the two has to do with how data is stored. Static RAM will hold data as long as its powered up, while dynamic RAM must be refreshed every so often. But before we get into the details, take a look at Fig. 4-1, a block diagram of a typical static RAM.

STATIC RAM

There are three main parts to the static RAM IC: The memory-cell array; the address decoders, and the input/output (I/O) block. The heart of the device is the memory array (a matrix of storage cells). Each cell is capable of storing one bit of data (either a one or a zero). The actual construction of the cell depends on the logic being used, but the basic idea is the same for all families.

Figure 4-2 shows the basic storage principle; two

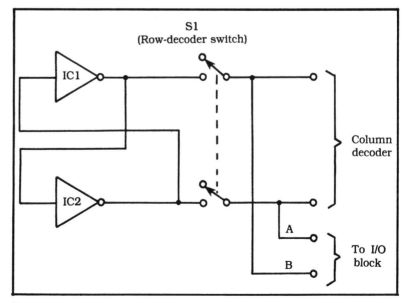

Fig. 4-2.

inverters are set up as simple latch with switches at the outputs to control read and write operations. The cells are arranged in a matrix. The number of rows and columns in the matrix are what determine the size of the memory.

When you want to do something to one cell, you put the address on the address bus, and the row and column decoders are used to close the switches surrounding the cell you've selected. The thing to note here is that as long as any cell remains unselected, it's not connected to anything; and whatever data you have there will stay there.

The same operation that picks a particular cell also connects it to the I/O logic in the IC, giving you the option of reading or writing data to that cell. Reading is simple because merely selecting the cell connects it to the I/O block and the data that's there to be read.

Of course, the data from that cell has to be conditioned before it can be used in the real world, since the inverters used in each cell won't have enough punch. That conditioning takes the form of an amplifier called, naturally enough, the *sense amplifier*. That amplifier has a very high input-impedance so it doesn't load down the cell and run the risk of glitching the data that's already stored there.

Writing new data into memory is just as simple; select the location, set up the data, and then flash a write pulse to the IC. The "nuts and bolts" of it is really no different from writing to a home-made latch. Since the two outputs of the storage cell will always be opposite in sense (remember that it's just a simple latch), a write operation is accomplished by grounding the column decode lines.

Figure 4-3 is a simplified representation of what happens. To keep the design of the device as simple as possible, the column lines are used to carry the cell outputs to the I/O block. Data is read off one line, but both lines are needed to write. If you want to store a zero, you ground the A line and for a one, ground the B line.

The I/O block has a few other jobs to do as well. It selects the line that is to be grounded during a write, and

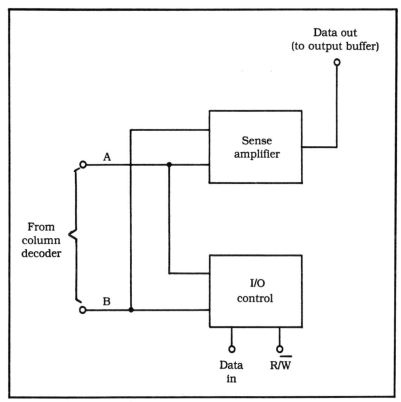

Fig. 4-3.

it also has the circuitry that controls the overall status of the IC. How extensive the block is depends on the particular memory you're using. Most RAM's have a CHIP ENABLE pin that will let the outputs be three-stated. That is important if you have several memories sharing the same data.

What other kinds of "goodies" you find in the I/O block depends on the logic technology the memory is using. CMOS memories have a low-power mode that lets you "put the chip to sleep," while saving all data. Some of the memories we'll be looking at need as little as 1 μA (or less) to save data! That should bring all sorts of battery-backup schemes to mind.

Memories that are organized to handle more than one bit at a time (256 × 4, 512 × 8, etc.) have to have a separate memory matrix for each data line. A 256 × 4 memory will be four arrays deep, and each of them will have its own set of I/O circuits. When you get to the point where you are stacking things eight layers deep, the design is getting really hairy and, as you would expect, it shows up in the price. That's why a 2048 × 1 memory is a lot cheaper than a 256 × 4. The total storage is the same but the complication of the internal design is much greater.

Static RAM's are easy to use; most modern designs are really forgiving of the the screw-ups that always manage to show up during breadboarding. When you start talking about dynamic RAM, however, all notions of friendliness have to be thrown out the window.

DYNAMIC RAM

Because of the way a dynamic RAM stores data, it can be a nightmare to use: Instead of nice stable inverters, it uses a single capacitor . . . and nothing else! (See Fig. 4-4.) Since the leakage time is usually measured in microseconds, some scheme is necessary to make sure that the data stored in memory stays put. That problem is solved by periodically rewriting the data in each cell. That process, called *refresh* is handled by the sense amplifier that's connected to each column.

When a row and column are selected, the first thing the sense amplifier does is to read the data from each cell in the row and then write it back in. Since only one column is selected, only that cell has its output channeled to the data bus. Every read, then, refreshes the entire row.

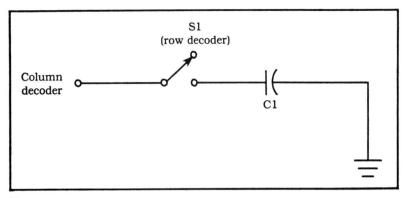

Fig. 4-4.

Modern RAM has built-in circuitry to refresh the entire IC during a read, and a whole row can be refreshed by just addressing it. However, that doesn't make refreshing any better—just a little bit easier!

Many popular dynamic RAM's use the same pin for both row and column addressing. Two control pins—the row and column strobes—are used to tell the RAM which addresses are on the bus. It's still up to us, however, to make sure that the right stuff is at the right place at the right time.

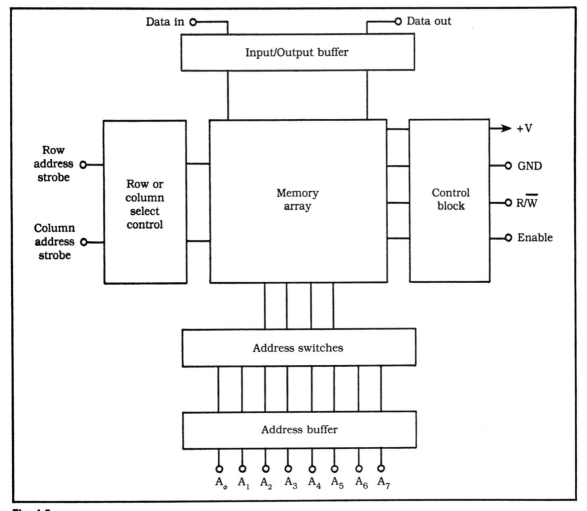

Fig. 4-5.

Figure 4-5 is a block diagram of a dynamic RAM and if you study it you'll be able to see how its pins relate to each other. Keep in mind that there's plenty of detail in the IC that has not been drawn in. If you're morbid enough to want to get into the anatomy of a dynamic RAM, you can find a complete diagram in any good databook.

The question that should come to mind at this time, however, is: Why in the world would anybody decide to use dynamic, rather than static, RAM? The answer is simple—it makes more economic sense: Because the cells are smaller, you can stuff more of them into the same size IC. That means that more memory is available for a lot less money.

By now you probably know more than you ever wanted to know about what goes on inside RAM . . . and believe me when I tell you that there's a lot more we could talk about. But, being practical minded, let's end the whole discussion here. After all, what we're interested in is not so much how those things work, but how we can use them.

Over the next few pages we'll see how memory IC's can cut "brain-blasting" circuit hassles down to nothing, and we'll also design some circuits that you can adapt for your own purposes. You'll find that memories are good for a lot more than just remembering! And if you want to use huge amounts of memory, we'll design refresh circuitry that cannot only handle any amount of memory you want, but is completely transparent as well.

So that you can get ready for it, let me remind you of a short corollary to Grossblatt's eighteenth rule: Get it in writing. In other words, pick up a databook containing the specifications for both *static* and *dynamic* RAM. The timing diagrams are invaluable design aids and are sure to prove their worth.

You'll find that having well-drawn timing diagrams in front of you as you're working is the only known cure for the dreaded memory disease known as "electronic amnesia" or more technically, "silicon senility."

The advantage of the latter is that we can make our system operate exactly as if we had 512 bytes of continuous memory. If you think about the problem for a moment, it becomes obvious that the key to banking the memory is careful use of each IC's enable pins. Only one bank can be enabled at any one time or the whole system will go up in smoke. What we have to find is a trigger that we can use to switch between banks automatically.

The best trigger is the address of the desired location. We'll assign Bank 1 addresses from 000 to 0FF (0 to 255 decimal), and Bank 2 addresses from 100 to 1FF (256 to 511 decimal). Now our problem is well defined. Any address placed on the bus that's less than or equal to 0FF will automatically access Bank 1, and any address above that will access Bank 2. As you can see, our problem in memory management has turned into a problem in simple logic design.

The easiest way to accomplish the desired bank selection is shown in Fig. 4-7. Since we have a 512-byte system ($512 = 2^9$), there will be 9 address lines. Any address above 0FF will place a high level on the most significant bit, so that's what we'll use to select between our two banks. The 5101 has three *Chip Enable* pins (17, 18, and 19), but from examination of that IC, they do different things to the IC.

Pin 17 switches between normal and low-power standby operation; pin 18 enables the outputs; and pin 19 enables the IC as a whole. In our circuit we want to control the entire IC, since when a bank is switched off we want to inhibit both reads and writes. A look at the

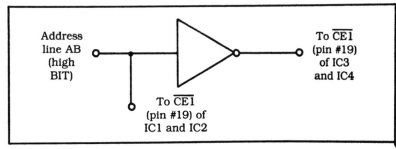

Fig. 4-7.

IC's data sheet reveals that we have to keep pin 17 high, pin 18 low, and we must use the high address (A9) line to control pin 19.

The inverter in Fig. 4-7 does the bank switching for us. When Bank 1 is selected, Bank 2 is deselected. And it's all done automatically.

If you want to add memory to the system, you can build on that technique. The only limitation is the width of the address bus. We've got to have a spare address line around to do the switching for us. However, nothing stays simple forever.

Consider this scenario: You have a 64K memory system that's controlled by an eight-bit microprocessor. Consequently, all the address lines are used to do real addressing. Suppose you want to add some more memory to the system. There are several reasons for doing that:

- As an alternate 64K bank for data storage, etc.
- To increase continuous memory in the system to 128K.

The problem then is to control the memory when the address bus is limited to sixteen bits (2^{16} = 65,536), or 64K. And *that* as you know, is a real problem.

MORE ON MEMORY MANAGEMENT

Anyone who has ever built a system that uses memory for one thing or another should be familiar with the truth of Grossblatt's Twelfth Law: *There's no such thing as too much memory.*

No matter how much memory you design into your system, it's a foregone conclusion that you'll wind up using all of it, and when you do, you'll start looking for ways to increase it. It's like buying a new house. I know many guys who swore they'd never need more than eight rooms. Two years later they had finished the attic and the basement, and they were eyeballing the garage!

Unfortunately, it takes more than a hammer and some nails to add more memory to an electronics system.

And it's slightly difficult to add memory to a system that's already using the full width of its address bus. There are several ways to solve that problem, and each has unique advantages and disadvantages. We'll use the circuit we put together last time to examine one solution; others are certainly possible.

You'll recall that, since we're dealing with 512 bytes of memory space, the address bus is nine bits wide. We use the most significant address bit to select one of two 256-byte banks of memory automatically, and that gives us 512 bytes of continuous memory. Let's assume, for purposes of discussion, that our memory system is managed by a controller that has an eight-bit *data* bus, a nine-bit *address* bus, as well as the usual set of read, write, control, and I/O signals. Given those parameters, let's see what we have to do to add more memory to the circuit.

MEMORY BANKING

No matter how you implement the circuit, the basic

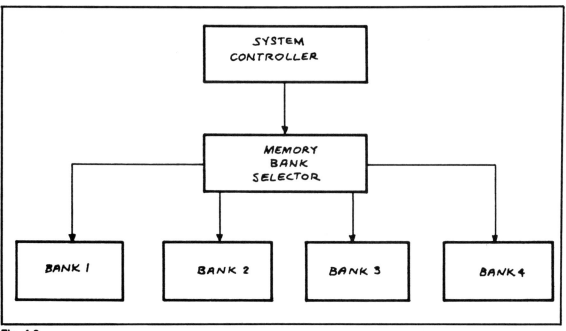

Fig. 4-8.

idea is to "page" or "bank" additional memory into the system. To understand the idea of bank-selecting memory, take a look at Fig. 4-8. Since our basic system can deal directly with only 512 bytes of memory, each page of memory will have 512 bytes. But in order for us to access different pages, we need a signal that the system can use to generate appropriate page-select signals. This time, there's no handy-dandy address line to do the job for us. But, even though we have to look elsewhere for an answer, the problem is basically the same. We need some sort of switch to toggle from one page to another.

The whole problem of getting from one bank of memory to another is one that computer designers face all the time. For example, any eight-bit computer that features 128K of memory uses some scheme to switch between two 64K banks.

You could always do the job with mechanical switches, but that's a bit rude and crude. A much better way is to use "soft switches" to do the toggling for us. "Soft switching" is a term that computer people use all the time; it represents a technique that we've used over and over in the circuits we've put together. All it means is that we put a decoder on the address bus and let it watch for a particular address. When that address shows up, the soft switch detects it and changes the state of its output.

As with any other problem in logic design, the first two steps are to decide exactly what you want to do and then to draw a good block diagram of the circuit. So, first, let's say that we want to piggy-back four banks of memory and have our new circuitry select the desired bank by flipping a couple of soft switches.

Second, the block diagram in Fig. 4-9 indicates the three basic elements we'll need: The *detector* senses the address we're looking for and causes the *decoder* to put out a signal that we can then *latch* to control our system. Now that we know what we need, let's see what we have to do to build it.

The detector is a snap—we've put together many of them during the last few years. You can use anything from a simple gates-only approach to dedicated decoder

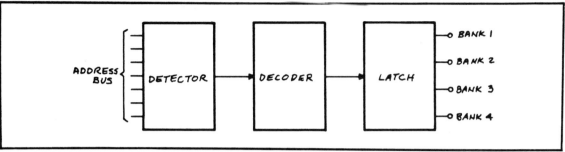

Fig. 4-9.

chips. Since we're just starting to find out how to build and use soft switches, let's take the most straightforward design approach. After we've got the system working, we'll see what we can do to simplify things.

Memory is addressed in our system from 000 to 1FF. We have to pick four addresses to use as our soft-switch locations. In a real-world system there would probably be circuit considerations that would dictate which locations to use. But since we're building our circuit from the ground up, we can pick any addresses we want. Let's take the four highest addresses in the system and define them according to the table shown in Fig. 4-10A. As you can see, the highest address (1FF) selects the first page, 1FE selects the second page, and so on.

A starting point for the circuit we need is shown in Fig. 4-10B. Since the four addresses we're looking for are all at the top of memory, the seven most significant lines will all be high when one of those addresses is accessed. That means we can use an eight-input NAND gate as the front end of our circuit. So, any time the NAND gate outputs a low, our circuit is addressing one of the soft switches. The two least significant bits of the address bus (A0 and A1) will determine which bank of our memory system to enable.

Since we only want to enable one bank at a time, the second part of our circuit has to be a one-of-four decoder. There are several IC's we could use, but it's always a good idea to keep the idea of system expansion in mind. The 4051 shown in Fig. 4-10 is a one-of-eight switch that we've used here before. It's a CMOS analog switch that can handle either analog or digital signals; the digital

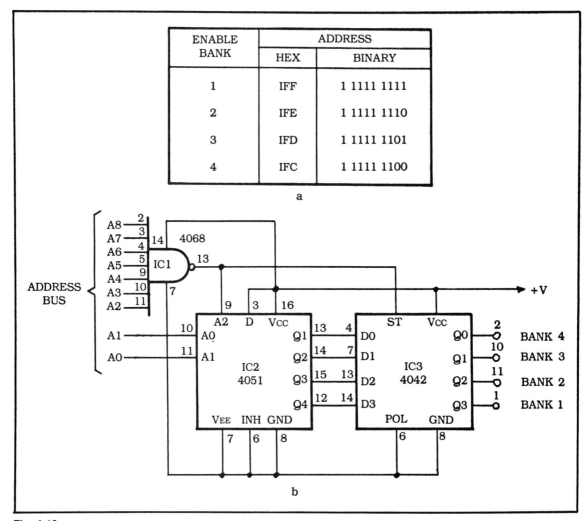

ENABLE BANK	ADDRESS	
	HEX	BINARY
1	IFF	1 1111 1111
2	IFE	1 1111 1110
3	IFD	1 1111 1101
4	IFC	1 1111 1100

a

b

Fig. 4-10.

mode is selected by tying pin 7 low. The data presented to the D input at pin 3 is transferred to the output selected by the A0-A2 inputs (pins 9-11). Since we're decoding four banks of memory with two inputs, we'll use the most significant select line (A2) to enable the IC.

The last part of the circuit is a latch. The 4042 is a four-bit latch with a really neat feature. We can make it latch data on either a high or a low trigger by tying the POLARITY input (pin 6) high or low. The signal from the NAND gate is active low, so we'll tie the POLARITY pin low.

So, whenever a low is presented to the STORE input (pin 5), the data at the latch's inputs will be stored. They'll also appear at the latch's outputs.

The circuit works like this: When one of our soft-switch addresses shows up on the system address bus, the output of the NAND gate goes low. That allows the 4051 to transfer that signal to the output selected by address lines A0 and A1. Since a low is also presented to the STORE input of the 4042, the state of the four 4051 outputs are latched and transferred to the memory enable lines. The result: the selected bank is enabled and the other three banks are disabled.

CAVEATS

There are a few considerations you should keep in mind when using that arrangement, or a similar one, to control a banked memory system. First, you'll notice that there's no way of predicting which states the latch's output lines will be in when the system is first powered up. Zero, one, or even several of the memory banks could be enabled when you first apply power. That last possibility exists because the 4051 can have an illegal output state—more than one high output—if much noise is present at power up.

Previously, when we were faced with that sort of problem, we used an RC network to generate a quick-and-dirty reset pulse to make sure that things were set up the way we wanted them. But if you examine our circuit, you'll see that it is, unfortunately, too complicated for that type of reset. A simple reset pulse just won't work since there are so many variables involved. A hardware reset would have to control all the circuit elements, so it would be very difficult to design. But there are other ways to solve that problem.

BANK-SWITCHING

Except for the addition of resistors R1-R4, the circuit shown in Fig. 4-11 here is quite similar to the circuit shown in Fig. 4-10. We'll discuss why we need the

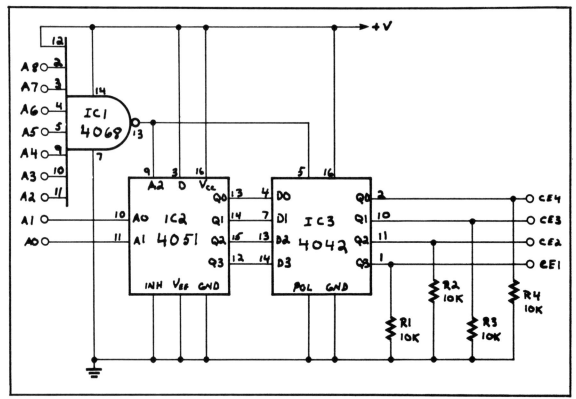

Fig. 4-11.

resistors below; for now let's look at the circuit just in terms of logic.

Since the CMOS data selector we're using is a 4051, we can send either a high or a low to the selected output (Q1-Q4), depending on what the 4051's DATA input (pin 3) is connected to. In this case, it is connected to the positive supply rail.

When the high-order address line (A2-A8) are high, IC1's output goes low. Then, depending on the state of A0 and A1, a high will be fed to one of the outputs of the 4051. That high will be clocked into four-bit latch IC2. That signal provides an active-high memory-enable signal.

ACTIVE-HIGH OR ACTIVE-LOW?

Each of the four banks of our memory system is made up of four 5101's. The pins in Fig. 4-6 should be marked

$\overline{CE1}$. The active-low *vs* active-high issue wasn't important there (Fig. 4-6), but adding additional banks as we're doing now requires careful attention to the level of the enabling signal.

That aside, if you examine the circuit, you'll see that we're doing memory banking there as well. Each bank is composed of two IC's, and the $\overline{CE1}$ pin of each IC is used for bank selection. Our circuit uses a nine-bit address bus; the high bit of that bus allows us to switch 256-byte banks transparently, yielding a 512-byte system.

What we want to do now is add three additional 512-byte banks to the system. To do that, we'll have to use the 5101's other enable pins. If the IC had only one enable pin, we'd be faced with a fairly complex gating problem, but, fortunately for us, the 5101 has *three* separate enable pins.

We use pin 19 to select a 256-byte page in a bank, so we'll use pin 17 to select the bank as a whole (512 bytes). If that sounds confusing, it may help you to think of each 512-byte page as a separate section.

If you bring pin 17 of the 5101 low, the IC "goes to sleep." Actually, it goes into a low-power mode in which all data are retained and power requirements are reduced to less than 10 microamps. So, by using pin 17 as a bank selector, we get reduced current drain as a freebie! The point is that the banking circuit must put a high on the enable pin of the bank we want to select and a low on all the others. That's why we tie the DATA input (pin 3) of the 4051 high.

The reason we need resistors R1-R4 is to ensure that the memory's enable pins are in a well-defined state. We wouldn't want those pins to float; data in the RAM might be garbled if the IC were accidentally accessed for even a brief period of time. Since we need active-*high* enable signals, we need to use pull-*down* resistors.

To use the bank-switching circuit shown here with the memory circuit shown in Fig. 4-6, tie pin 17 from all 5101's in each bank together and connect that line to one of the CE outputs of the circuit shown here. That gives us four banks of memory, each of which is selectable by flipping a soft switch located at an address ranging from 1FC to 1FF.

How can we select a memory bank? And how can we initialize the system properly? Those questions are interrelated, as we'll see. It would be difficult to generate a reset signal that would ensure that only one bank was enabled at power up. However, if we use our Z80 circuit as the system controller, the solution to the problem is simple.

When we designed the Z80 system, we made sure there was an RC-generated reset pulse produced at power-up. Among other things, that forces the Z80 to begin execution at location 0000. That being the case, to initialize the system all we have to do is have the Z80 flip one of the soft switches before it tries to access any RAM. To do that, the Z80 can execute any instruction that causes the address of the soft switch to be put on the address bus. The system's hardware will take over the task from that point.

Any of the Z80's "load" instructions is a good choice. For example, if the first instruction in your program is LD A, (01FF), the Z80 will obligingly put 01FF on the address bus and cause our circuit to enable one of the memory banks. Believe it or not, that's all you have to do to flip a soft switch. And it doesn't matter which instruction is used as long as it results in the appearance of a soft switch's address on the bus.

OTHER USES

We mentioned last time that there are several ways to set up alternate banks of memory in a system. Soft switches are a neat way to organize memory, but they can be used for other things as well. And there are other ways of generating banking signals too. Let's look at some of those.

For example, if you're using only seven bits of data, you could use the eighth bit as a select line. Set the bit to talk to one bank of memory, and reset it to talk to the other. A more reasonable alternative would be to use an otherwise-unused Z80 control signal—an unused address line, perhaps, would serve well.

An externally generated signal may be a good choice in some systems. For example, if you're sensing and recording real-world data, some predetermined condition could be used to switch memory banks. For example, suppose you connected the bank switching system to a low-battery or power-failure alarm. A signal produced by a circuit of that kind could cause data to be transferred from volatile dynamic memory to battery-backed-up CMOS RAM. And yes, it's perfectly reasonable to mix two different memory types in one system.

Using that sort of scheme to capture data is a common practice. Commercial airlines, for example, use it in flight recorders, and a similar setup is used by recorders for unattended remote data gathering.

There are a few things to keep in mind when you set up a banked-memory system. The IC's you use in your switch circuitry must match or exceed your system's operating speed. The CMOS NAND gate we used is slow—about 150 nanoseconds. You could use a high-speed CMOS or TTL part to increase that speed by about a factor of 10.

If you're really interested in microprocessor system design, put the circuit together and connect it to the Z80 demo system we've been discussing. Of course, the Z80 has a 16-bit address bus, so switching 512-byte banks of memory is unnecessary, but you'll learn a great deal by making the system work. And that knowledge could be put to real-world use by designing a banking system that switches between 64K banks—and a memory system of that sort can be very useful.

WHICH MEMORY?

We recently spent a lot of time talking about the different kinds of memory: what they were, how they worked, and how to use them. The two basic types of RAM, static and dynamic, each have characteristics that are particularly useful for specific applications. Which type of memory you should use depends on the kind of circuit that you want to put together. As with most things in life, there's a trade-off involved; you have to weigh the amount of memory you need against the amount of effort you will have to put into the design of the circuit.

There's no getting around the fact that static RAM is a whole lot easier to use than dynamic RAM. When you put data in a static RAM, you can forget about it. Just about the only thing you have to do to guarantee that the data will be there when you want it is to keep the power turned on; and if you refer to our previous discussion of low-power CMOS memory, you'll see that there are ways of making sure your data is there even when the power is turned off.

One of the oldest rules of circuit design is summed up very neatly in Grossblatt's fifth law: "Always keep brain damage to a minimum." But you'll occasionally run afoul of Grossblatt's twelfth law, which is: "There's no such thing as too much memory." It's sad, but true, that there comes a time in the life of every circuit designer when they're forced by circumstances to turn away from the relatively hassle-free world of static RAM and enter the hassle-full world of dynamic RAM. If your circuit needs megabytes of memory, if your power supply starts heating up, or if you're just running out of board space, you'll find it impossible to meet all of your storage requirements with static RAM.

The characteristic that makes dynamic RAM such a hassle to use is also the same one that makes it so attractive. Of course, I'm talking about *refreshing*. Before we get into the nuts and bolts of circuit design, let's spend a bit of time examining the anatomy of a standard dynamic RAM.

The basic memory cells in a dynamic RAM are much smaller and less complex than those of a static RAM, which results in more storage for the same size package. Since it's one thing to describe the difference between the two of them, but another thing to actually see them side by side, Fig. 4-12 shows how the complexity of a typical static RAM cell compares with that of a dynamic RAM cell. Whereas the static RAM usually consists of two cross-coupled inverters, the dynamic RAM, as you can see from Fig. 4-12, is nothing more than a small capaci-

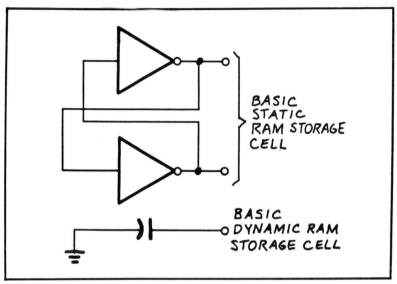

BASIC
STATIC
RAM STORAGE
CELL

BASIC
DYNAMIC RAM
STORAGE CELL

Fig. 4-12.

tor directly on the IC's substrate. (By using techniques such as address multiplexing, we can increase the number of directly-addressable cells without increasing the size of the IC's package.)

When a chip designer sits down to work out the internal circuitry of an IC, there are a few basic rules he follows, and one of them is to minimize the number of passive components. The space on an IC's substrate is limited, and passive components take up a lot of room. It's true that a small capacitor takes up less room on the substrate than the transistors needed to make the two inverters found in a static RAM cell, but the operative word there is "small."

SMALL MEANS SHORT

We have all used capacitors for temporary storage, but if you look over your old designs you'll notice that most stand-alone storage capacitors have values in the microfarad range; they are usually the electrolytic type. The reason for using large-value capacitors is simple—you want the longest time constant you can possibly get. Although the exact value of the capacitors used for dynamic RAM varies from IC to IC, you can get

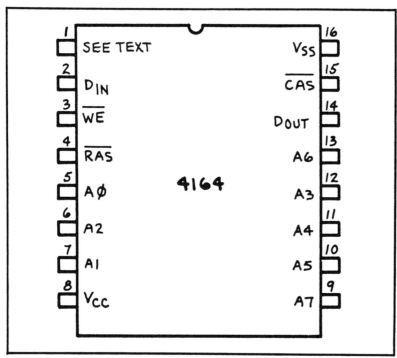

Fig. 4-13.

an approximate idea of that value by considering that the integrity of the data stored there can only be guaranteed for 2 milliseconds!

Since the data will disappear in 2 milliseconds, the circuit-designer must provide memory-support circuitry that will periodically read out the data in every single cell and write it back in. That process, known as *refresh*, is a basic fact of dynamic RAM life.

If you're used to dealing with static memory, the first feature of the 4164 you should notice is that (Fig. 4-13) there are only 8 address pins, A0 through A7. Ordinarily, this wouldn't be enough for decoding the 65,536 memory cells on the substrate, but you'll remember that I had mentioned the notion of "address multiplexing." The address pins are used in conjunction with RAS, (*Row Address Strobe*) and CAS, (*Column Address Strobe*) to provide a complete address. When you want to access a particular location in the IC, the row address is presented to the address pins and the RAS pin is strobed,

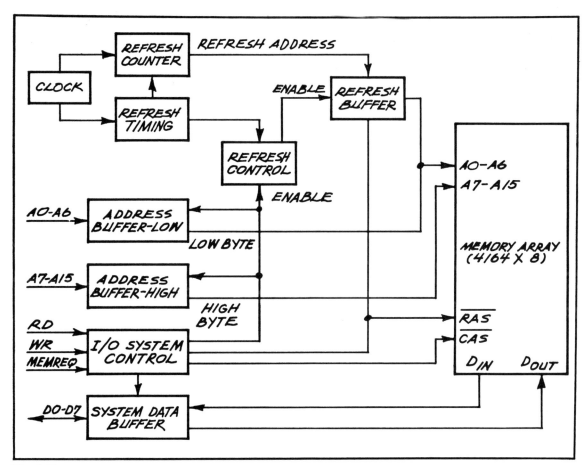

Fig. 4-14.

which causes the partial address to be internally latched in the IC. The column address is then presented to the same address pins and the CAS pin is strobed to internally latch the remainder of the complete address.

If all that wasn't enough, the issue of refresh has to be dealt with as well. And there are other peculiarities of dynamic RAM that I haven't even mentioned.

The logical glue that has to be added to the board before it can be used for anything is what made me call our project a "system." But the complications don't really make anything any harder, only more interesting.

DYNAMIC MEMORY

Up until about eight or nine years ago, systems

designers would avoid dynamic memory like the plague. The reason for that was simple: the disadvantages far outweighed the advantages. You could plop static RAM in a circuit and use it without much other thought, but dynamic RAM required a lot of support circuitry. In fact, back in those days a 16K dynamic RAM was a big deal: it needed three supply voltages and was very particular about timing.

THINGS HAVE CHANGED

Today's cheap 64K dynamic RAM's are much easier to use and, since they give so many bits for the buck, any designer worth his salt has to be familiar with them. Lots of special dynamic RAM controllers are available that take care of all of a dynamic RAM's special needs, and make them almost as easy to use as static RAM. To help you get a good grasp on how to use dynamic RAM, we'll put together a simple system; and although the system won't be state-of-the-art, once you understand how it works you'll have a good grasp on the basic considerations of designing with dynamic RAM.

Keeping in mind the DRAM (*D*ynamic *R*andom *A*ccess *M*emory) characteristics we discussed, you can see that any system using them has to have certain building blocks. The block diagram in Fig. 4-14 describes not only the system we're putting together, but also one that uses the most sophisticated LSI DRAM controller. The difference between the two is where the elements are found. A lot of the discreet parts we'll be using are packed together in the substrate of LS1 devices such as Intel's 8208 family. Once you're familiar with our system, putting together an LSI system will be a relatively easy task.

The system has three main sections, and although each one does a separate job, they have to interact as well.

1. The memory array: That section contains only the actual storage devices. In our circuit it's made up of eight 4164's, each of which is organized as 64K × 1 bit.

2. The refresh circuit: That produces the control signals, sequential addresses, and the timing logic to maintain the data in the memory array.
3. The I/O circuitry: That circuitry generates the necessary timing and control signals to let an external device get access to the memory array.

Let's look at each of the sections individually.

FIRST SECTION

You should be familiar with the memory array because we've already spent lots of time talking about dynamic RAM in general and 4164's in particular. Each of the eight IC's has its address and control lines bused together. The DATA IN and DATA OUT pins on each IC are also tied together, because the direction of data flow will be controlled by the rest of the system, and the 4164 can be told to three-state its output.

SECOND SECTION

The refresh circuitry is designed to count systematically through all the addresses needed to maintain the stored data. That is, of course, the big drawback of using dynamic RAM. IC designers have made refresh as easy as possible and, if you read a 4164 data sheet, you'll see that there are several ways in which it can be done. We'll be doing a *RAS-only refresh*, which means that we present a row address to the A0 to A6 address pins of the memory array and then bring the RAS line low. That will automatically refresh all the memory cells located in that row.

A 4164's memory matrix is organized as 128 rows by 512 columns, so it's only necessary to sequence through 128 addresses to completely refresh the device. We're using 7 address lines (A0 to A6), because two to the seventh is 128. On the simplest level, refresh is done by putting out a 7-bit-address and strobing RAS, but there are other things to deal with as well. As we'll see, timing is the really critical factor and the state of the other memory-control pins has to be considered as well.

THIRD SECTION

The last section of our circuit handles the I/O. It's all well and good to build a system that can properly massage dynamic RAM, but it's not much good unless there's some way to store and access the data in the RAM. Any system wanting access to our circuit only has to give it an address, data, and a read or write request, and then sit back until it's notified that the job is done. Doing that with static RAM is simple, but the constant refresh activity that is going on in a dynamic RAM system complicates things.

Servicing a memory request means accessing a location somewhere in the memory array's address space. The chances are slight that the requested location is going to be on the row that's currently being refreshed; and it would take too long, and require a lot of extra circuitry, to wait until the refresh circuitry reaches the particular row containing the requested location. An external memory request means that the refresh activity has to be halted, access has to be given to the requested location, and then the refresh circuit can regain control of the memory.

If you're beginning to think that here is a real nightmare for a circuit designer, you're starting to appreciate and understand the reservations that most circuit people have about using dynamic RAM. Given all the needs of our system, putting one together with a gates-only approach would be extremely complex, even if the job were done using MSI components.

One of the major problems when dealing with dynamic RAM is the strict timing parameters. A standard 4164 will retain the data stored in its pint-sized capacitor cells for only 2 milliseconds. That means that your circuit has to perform a refresh on each cell within 2 milliseconds or the data is lost.

Since a RAS-type refresh works on a whole row at a time, and since there are 128 rows in a 4164, the refresh must be performed at least every 16 microseconds. The circuit that takes care of all that for you must be designed to sequence through several steps for each refresh operation.

1. The refresh counter has to increment to the next address.
2. That address has to be put on the address bus for the RAM.
3. A RAS signal has to be generated and fed to all the RAM.

TIMING IS IMPORTANT

As you can see, the sequence and timing of those steps have to be done properly if you want the system to work. And all that we've been talking about so far is the refresh operation. Somewhere in there we have to allow for the time needed for data to be stored to, or read from, the memory. After all, that's the whole reason for building the system in the first place.

The interaction between all the components of a dynamic memory system has to be carefully controlled in order for the circuit to work properly. Refresh has to be constant, and memory access has to be kept to a short operation that won't interfere with maintaining the data. Since a gates-only solution to the problem is so complex as to be impractical, it's obvious we have to look elsewhere for a way to handle all the problems.

Although we can use LSI controllers, they are expensive and hard to locate. The route we're going to follow should already have crossed your mind. Since we're putting together a complex system in which timing and access are the major problems, we can use a microprocessor to handle the job.

MICROPROCESSOR CONTROL

The Z-80 is the perfect CPU for the job. It has many memory-control signals as well as built-in circuitry especially designed for controlling dynamic RAM. An internal refresh counter will automatically provide the sequential addressing we need to take care of refresh, and the address is put on the bottom of the address bus during the tail end of each op code fetch.

The beauty of that scheme is that the Z-80 doesn't have any need for the address bus once it's loaded the op code. During portions of the instruction cycle the memory is idle. That gives us the time we need to use the address to refresh the RAM. Since the Z-80 is busy elsewhere during that time, it doesn't have to slow down or wait for the refresh operation to be carried out.

Section 5:
SEQUENCING, DISPLAY CIRCUITS, AND SPECIAL PURPOSE IC'S

THIS PARTICULAR SECTION PRESENTS VARIOUS MEANS OF retrieving data in a sequence, assorted methods of obtaining a hexadecimal display with LED's and a thorough examination of the IC called a rate multiplier.

AUTOMATIC DATA SEQUENCING

We've taken care of keyboard data entry with a binary keyboard encoder. This time, we'll see what must be added to that circuit to make it do something useful. After all, what good is the encoder without having some way of storing and/or manipulating its output data.

Since one of the design criteria is automatic sequencing of the address and data, we'll need something in the circuit that automatically does one thing after another. The problem of data sequencing is the binary keyboard encoder, which was designed to continuously scan a series of switches in search of a depressed key.

AUTOMATIC SEQUENCING SCHEME

Since we'll be sequencing both address and data, we

also need some way to let the circuit know which is which. The easiest way to keep track of what's stored where is to store the low and high order halves of the address, plus the data separately. Given all that, let's take a look at Fig. 5-1, a tentative solution to the problem.

The data coming out of the keyboard are fed to a series of latches, each of which is four bits wide. Since the 5101 (the static RAM that we'll be using for storage) has eight address pins and four data inputs, we'll need three latches to handle the job. You can get IC's that are 4-bit latches, but a "neater" way is to use a 4508. It's a 24-pin IC that is really two 4-bit hold-and-follow latches in one package. By using that IC, we'll only need two 4508's and have one latch left over for any brainstorms we might come up with in the future.

The easiest way to sequence things is to use a 4017 binary counter, an IC you should really become familiar

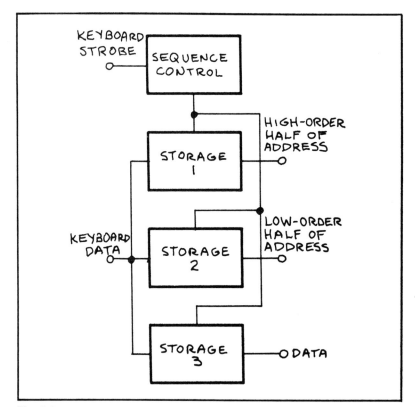

Fig. 5-1.

with. Now that we have the cast of characters for this portion of the circuit, let's put them together and see how they fit into our design.

How It Works

Figure 5-2 is a schematic of the circuit we'll use to sequence the binary information from the keyboard encoder. It consists of a 4017 counter/driver and two 4508 dual 4-bit latches.

The action of the 4017 is (or should be) self explanatory. One thing that does deserve a bit of attention, however, is the way the clocking is being done. The 4017 sequences on the positive going (ground to +V) half of the incoming clock pulse.

Note that the four data lines (0-3) of the 4017 are connected to the STROBE inputs of the latches. That is done to sequentially enable each latch. Also notice that the DISABLE pins of each latch is tied to ground: That means that the outputs of the 4508's are permanently enabled. However, there is no data output unless the strobe input is high.

The 4508 can provide a three-state output, but there is no need for it because there's no common output-bus. Each latch will be used to control different parts of the memory and will, therefore, be connected to different pins. (But keep the three-state option in mind because many applications require that feature, which is not found on all latches.)

When power is turned on, all four latches are cleared by the R-C pulse generated by R3 and C2. Also at turn-on, pin 3 (output "0") of the 4017 goes high and enables the inputs of the first latch. The circuit then sits there and waits patiently for you to press a key on the keyboard. In other words, any data presented to the input of IC5 will now be transferred to its output.

When a key is pressed, encoded data enters IC5-a and is passed on to its outputs (which is connected to 4 address inputs on the 5101 CMOS static RAM). At the same time, the strobe line goes from high to low and remains in that state so long as the switch is held down.

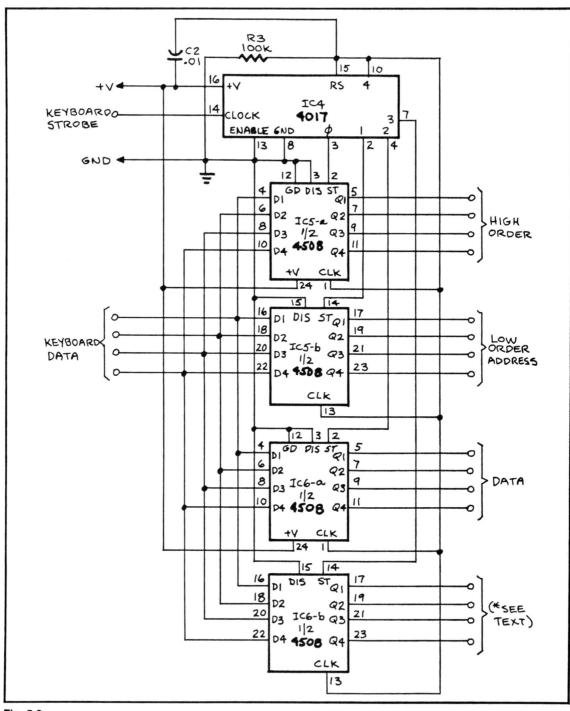

Fig. 5-2.

After the key is released, the strobe line returns to the high state and the 4017 advances by one count. That disables the first latch (IC5-a) and enables IC5-b, the next latch in the chain. The same action is repeated for each successive latch.

When putting the circuit together (and you should), note that the 4017 counts on the release of the switch rather than on the pressing of the switch. You could make things happen when the key is first pressed if you want, but it would take a bit more hardware and, quite honestly, I can't think of one reason for doing things that way.

When data comes off the keyboard, they are sequentially stored in each latch automatically. Now, automation is a wonderful thing, but there are times when you want a little more control. In our case, automation means that there's no way to go back. Put another way, if you hit the wrong key, there's no way to correct it. That's the penalty you pay for not designing things to work with an "enter" key.

If you feel that you'd like to be able to go back, or you want to actually strobe the data into the latch separately, all you have to do is put a clear switch into the circuit, or clock the 4017 with a separate switch. How to go about doing such things is a good exercise to see if you really have a clear understanding of all the things we've done so far. Design it yourself and try it out. As for me, I'm all in favor of automation.

When you add extra features to the circuit, keep in mind all the design rules we've discussed. Write everything down, from the criteria to the actual hardware you're putting in the circuit. As I said before, bad habits are hard to break, and any circuits designed with bad habits have a way of going up in smoke!

You'll notice that we have an extra latch left over. Since all we're handling is four data-bits and eight address-bits, the last latch seems to be an unavoidable waste of hardware. Why not put in some brain burning time; see if you can think of some use for it?

CLEVER HEXADECIMAL DISPLAY CIRCUITS

Obviously, many of you are interested in how to display hex values, so I'm going to take off from our discussion of the Z80 and devote this column to reporting some of the solutions. But before I go any further, let me remind you that I can't mention everybody's name or describe everybody's solution. Basically, the solutions I've received fall into three categories:

- A. Using special display IC's.
- B. Using elaborate decoding logic.
- C. Using PROM's for decoding.

DEDICATED IC'S

There are several dedicated IC's that do the job. Using the Motorola MC14495, which is a display decoder/driver that does just what we need: It decodes four-bit binary data into the correct output to drive seven-segment, common-cathode LED displays. Using this IC is no more complicated than using a 4511, or other common devices. The MC14495 is a CMOS device, so it may be used with supply voltages ranging from 4.5 to 16 volts dc. In addition, it has built-in current-limiting resistors, making the MC14495 an elegant solution to our problem.

So, you may well ask, if the MC14495 is so wonderful, why not use it? There is no problem when buying it in large quantities. But trying to find it in hobbyist quantities is murder. None of the regular mail-order houses advertise it, and when you do find it, the price is too steep to make using the 14495 worthwhile.

The Fairchild 9368, is another one-IC solution. The 9368 also drives seven-segment, common-cathode displays, but has no built-in current limiting resistors. However, it is easily available, and costs just over $3.00 in small quantities.

GATES-ONLY SOLUTIONS

I was really impressed by some of the gates-only designs sent in. Doing a gates-only solution to a complex logic problem can be a tedious job. And no matter how elegant your solution, there's always another one just a bit more elegant hovering around the corner. But whatever solution you arrive at, if it works, you should be proud of yourself.

Use a standard decoder/driver (like the 7448) to drive the display for inputs from 0000 to 0111, and additional circuitry to drive the display for inputs from 1000 to 1111. The trick is to use the high bit of the input word to disable the display driver IC for inputs greater than or equal to 1000.

Hook a 7404 inverter to the D input (pin 6) of a 7448, and feed the output to the BLANKING INPUT (pin 4) of that IC. So for any input greater than 0111, the D input goes high, the 7404 goes low, and the IC is disabled. Then the display LED may be driven with other circuitry. But be careful. You might confuse turning off the display with three-stating it. In the case of a 4511, for example, a blank display means that the outputs are all low—and that's a far cry from being three- stated!

Since you'll drive the display with additional decoders for inputs above 0111, you should isolate both driver sections with three-state buffers. If you don't, the operation of the whole circuit is going to be flaky at best and non-existent at worst.

You might go the data-selector and diodes route. That's like building your own PROM, and is a sensible way to solve logic problems when you're short on time, supplies, and patience. The circuit shown in Fig. 5-3 is an example of that kind of approach.

Circuit operation is simple. Each four-bit word at the input will cause one and only one of the 74154's outputs to go low. The segments of the display are driven by IC2, a 74LS244 octal buffer whose inputs are held high by 2.2K resistors R1 to R7. Any segment that's tied to a 74154 output through a diode will stay off when that output is selected.

There are both advantages and disadvantages to that sort of design. On the plus side, the format of the display of each digit can be changed simply by adding or removing diodes. In addition, the circuit can be put to-

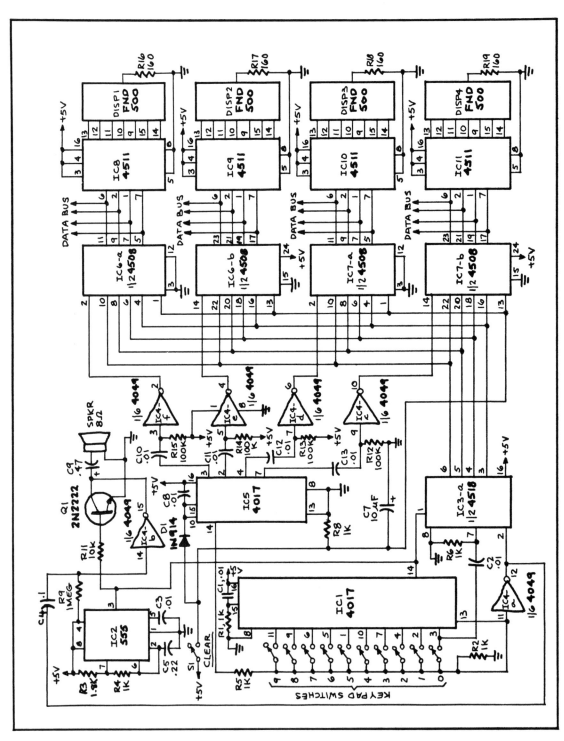

Fig. 5-3.

ᴦether from readily available parts for about 10
ᴦs—including perfboard and IC sockets. The
ᴦback is that the circuit takes a lot of connections.

ᴦROM APPROACH

ᴦsing a PROM was the most common solution to our
ᴦem. That approach is shown in Fig. 5-4A. The truth
ᴦto decode sixteen binary inputs has sixteen entries,
ᴦown in Fig. 5-4B. For such a small amount of data,
ᴦll PROM will suffice. You could burn the code into
ᴦROM, but the smallest one available is the 1K-by-8
ᴦ Since we only need sixteen bytes, using a 2708 is
ᴦing after a fly with an elephant gun.

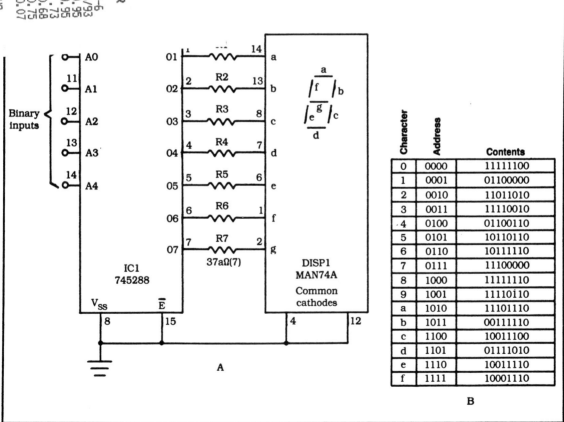

Character	Address	Contents
0	0000	11111100
1	0001	01100000
2	0010	11011010
3	0011	11110010
4	0100	01100110
5	0101	10110110
6	0110	10111110
7	0111	11100000
8	1000	11111110
9	1001	11110110
a	1010	11101110
b	1011	00111110
c	1100	10011100
d	1101	01111010
e	1110	10011110
f	1111	10001110

B

Fig. 5-4.

The best choice is probably a small bipolar PROM, such as the 74S288, which has a 32-word × 8-bit memory, costs about $2.00 in small quantities, and is available everywhere. The 74S288 is rather easy to program (as bipolar PROM's go).

See the truth table shown in Fig. 5-4B. Burning it in a 74S288 will give you a single-IC decoder/driver for common-cathode displays. But you've still got half the PROM to play with. You could make use of that by burning an inverted truth table in the upper half of the PROM. You would then have an IC that could drive either a common-anode or a common-cathode LED display. Select the one you want by using address input A4 (pin 14) as a selector. Tie it low to drive a common-cathode display, and tie it high to drive a common-anode display.

As you know, the problem with bipolar PROM's is getting them programmed. There are many programming services that will program bipolar PROM's for you. All you have to do is provide them with the code and the cash.

But designing a circuit to burn bipolar PROM's isn't very difficult. All the specifications are given in the data books, and the problem is just complex enough to be interesting.

SPECIAL-PURPOSE IC'S

Working alone in an isolated corner of the basement is great for the concentration, but there are certain inherent disadvantages. Floods and poor lighting, for example, go with the territory. However; the biggest problem is the isolation: It's impossible to keep up with *all* the literature and learn about all the latest time-saving devices if you remain tucked away in your cocoon. Furthermore, we all have a tendency to stick with familiar components—so certain IC's that could save us loads of design time never find their way onto the workbench.

Well, there are a couple of other IC's that can make certain design problems shrink from formidable to trivial. Even though they have been around for a long time, they are special-purpose IC's and, as such, can handle only the job for which they were designed. This time we're going to examine the *rate multiplier*, which is another type of special IC. We'll find out what it can do and how we can use it.

RATE MULTIPLIERS

One of the least understood special-purpose IC's in use today is the *rate multiplier*. This special-purpose counter, available in either CMOS or TTL versions, comes in two basic configurations—binary and BCD (*Binary-Coded Decimal*). Figure 5-5 lists some of the various rate multipliers available. To put it in simple terms, a rate multiplier is a number cruncher. It allows us to do all kinds of arithmetic from simple operations (like multiplication and division) to more complex functions (like logarithms and square roots). Which rate multiplier you use depends on the logic family you are using and the kind of counting you want to do.

There are minor differences between the TTL and CMOS versions, but we won't get into that until we have a better idea of what rate multipliers are all about. Because we need some starting place, we'll look at the CMOS binary version (4089).

Figure 5-6 shows the pinout for the 4089. In simple terms, a frequency is fed into the IC at the clock input (pin 9) and it, in turn, provides us with two kinds of outputs. The first (at pin 1) is called the BASE-RATE output. That output frequency is equal to the input clock divided by 16. The second output is at pin 6 (the complement of which is at pin 5): For want of an official

FAMILY	DEVICE	TYPE	MAXIMUM COUNT
TTL	7497	BINARY	64
TTL	74167	BCD	10
CMOS	4089	BINARY	16
CMOS	4527	BCD	10

Fig. 5-5.

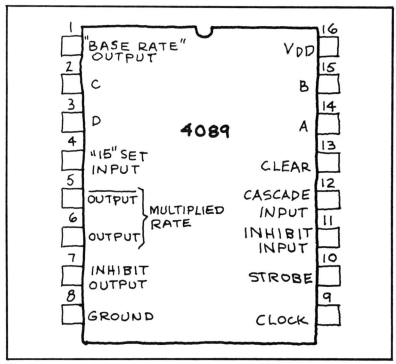

Fig. 5-6.

name, we'll refer to it as the MULTIPLIED RATE output. That output is equal to the base-rate frequency multiplied by whatever binary number is presented at its weighted inputs (at pins 14, 15, 2, and 3). If all that seems complicated at first, don't worry; you'll soon see that it really isn't.

The 4089 takes an input clock frequency and divides it internally by 16. The BASE-RATE output (at pin 1) will put out one pulse for every 16-pulses fed to the clock input at pin 9. The weighted inputs, pins 14, 15, 2, and 3, are preprogrammed to represent a numerical value (A = 1, B = 2, C = 4, and D = 8 respectively). Now let's assume we present a binary 5 or 0101 at the weighted inputs. In other words, a high A, low B, high C, and a low D is equal to 5. The multiplied output is going to be the base-rate multiplied by 5.

If a frequency of 16 kHz is fed to the clock input, the base-rate output will be 1 kHz. The frequency at the multiplied output then becomes 5 times that, or 5 kHz.

LOGIC STATE (ASSUMING 16 INPUT CLOCK PULSES)									NUMBER OF PULSES (OR LOGIC STATE)			
INPUT/PIN NUMBER									OUTPUT/PIN NUMBER			
D/3	C/2	B/15	A/14	INH/11	STR/10	CAS/12	CLR/13	SET/4	OUT/6	$\overline{OUT}$/5	INH/7	M.R./1
0	0	0	0						L	H		
0	0	0	1						1	1		
0	0	1	0						2	2		
0	0	1	1						3	3		
0	1	0	0						4	4		
0	1	0	1		HELD LOW FOR NORMAL OPERATION				5	5	ONE PULSE PER OUTPUT CYCLE DURING NORMAL OPERATION	
0	1	1	0						6	6		
0	1	1	1						7	7		
1	0	0	0						8	8		
1	0	0	1						9	9		
1	0	1	0						10	10		
1	0	1	1						11	11		
1	1	0	0						12	12		
1	1	0	1						13	13		
1	1	1	0						14	14		
1	1	1	1						15	15		
DOESN'T MATTER				1	0	0	0	0				
				0	1	0	0	0	L	H	1	1
				0	0	1	0	0	H	*	1	1
1				0	0	0	1	0	16	16	H	L
0				0	0	0	1	0	L	H	H	L
				0	0	0	0	1	L	H	L	H

Fig. 5-7.

The rest of the pins are used either to control the operation of the IC or to cascade several IC's together. The easiest way to understand what they do is to look at Fig. 5-7: There you see a complete listing of the various input possibilities along with their outputs. But before we go into the details of the device's operation, let's take a look at what was once called the *big picture*.

OUTPUT SYMMETRY

It sounds as though the IC is doing all kinds of useful things that we would ordinarily accomplish with a circuit board full of gates. Things, such as selectable frequency-division with nothing more than a clock, an IC, and a rotary switch is a wonderful idea. But take a look at the example we've just gone through. Everything seems to work out fine, but consider this: Let's suppose that the input clock isn't some convenient multiple of 16.

Let's see what's going to happen here if, for example, the input clock frequency is 17 kHz. Are you beginning to catch my drift? Obviously things are going to get really messy, because that would make the base rate 17,000/16, or 1062.5 Hz. Now, if we stick with a chosen rate of 5, the multiplied-rate output would be 1062.5 × 5 or 5312.5 Hz. Even that wouldn't be too bad—but there's another bit of nastiness that hasn't been mentioned yet.

The rate-multiplier is designed to output one base-rate pulse, plus the dialed-up number (the base rate multiplied by the number at weighted input) for every 16 pulses fed to the clock input. Now, if we look at the base rate on a scope, there's no problem. The pulses are evenly spaced and will track along at one-sixteenth the input clock-rate, but the multiplied rate is another story. Well, as we all know, 16 is not a multiple of 5. But we will see 5 pulses for every 16 incoming pulses . . . . . so what does that mean?

What it means is that the symmetry of the multiplied-rate pulses are out the window. Remember that the multiplied-rate output is tied to the incoming clock, not the base-rate output! The width of the multiplied-rate pulses will be the same as the incoming clock pulses, but

Section 6: USING THE 4017 AND 4018

DETAILING TWO USEFUL COUNTERS FOR THE HOBBYIST, THIS section covers such differences as the method of counting each employs and the idiosyncracies when using these IC's.

EXTENDING THE COUNTING RANGE OF THE 4017

The 4017 is one of the most popular of the CMOS MSI (*Medium Scale Integration*) counters. Because it sequences its outputs one at a time, it's ideally suited to serve as a frequency divider, pulse delayer, and so on. This IC even has a carry output that allows you to cascade as many 4017's as desired.

There is an application, however, where the use of the 4017 isn't quite as simple and straightforward. We're talking about connecting several of them together so that they will all sequence their outputs one IC after another. The carry output isn't any good here because it goes high for one-half of the IC's full count and low for the other half. That's great if you want a squarewave whose repetition rate is one-tenth of the input clock frequency.

But it doesn't help at all if you need a simple circuit that will take an input-clock signal and turn on more than ten outputs in sequence. Doing that requires a bit of external gating.

We will look at how you can arrange three 4017's to sequence in turn and provide up to twenty-five outputs with a minimum of external gating. We will be using a 4011 quad-NAND gate to achieve the desired gating arrangement. The same principle can be followed if you need more than twenty-five outputs; just add more 4017's and a few more gates. Since there are four NAND gates in the 4011, it will accommodate two more 4017's to give you a total of 41 outputs. We're losing five possible outputs for a variety of reasons that will become clear shortly.

How It Works

In Fig. 6-1, the clock inputs of all the 4017's are tied together so that they can all be triggered by a common clock pulse, and the same goes for the reset pins. The key to making the circuit work is using the gates to control the enable pins (pin 13) so that the three IC's can be made to count in sequence. Since the enable pins are active high, they have to be brought low. We'll use the NAND gates to control the order in which the 4017's are enabled.

When power is first applied to the circuit, capacitor C1 generates a reset pulse that forces all the 4017's to output a "1" at pin 3. One of the unfortunate features of the 4017 is the lack of a convenient inhibit pin that we could use to turn off all the outputs. When the enable pin is brought high it only disables the clock input—it doesn't do anything to the outputs. That's why we need the external gating and that's also the reason that we can only get 25 outputs from the circuit instead of 30.

When the counting first starts, pin 11 of all the counters is brought low. Because pin 11 of IC1 is connected to its enable pin, the IC is enabled and starts to count. That same low signal is fed to one leg of NAND gate IC4-a at pin 5 to control the enable pin of IC2. The other leg of the NAND gate, pin 6, is connected to IC2 pin

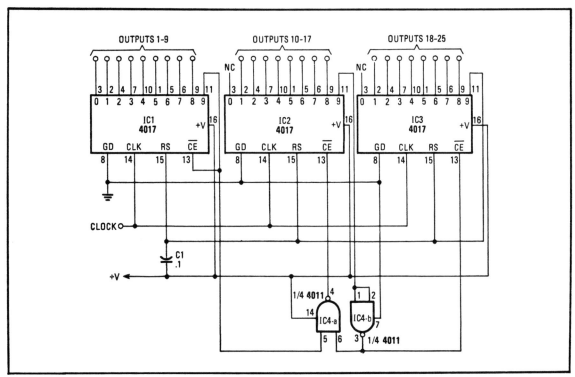

Fig. 6-1.

11 through IC4-b, which is used as an inverter. Because IC2 was reset at the start of the counting process, its output at pin 11 is also low. That low output is inverted by IC4-b and the resulting high output is applied to IC3 to disable it. The high output from IC4-b is also applied to IC4-a, which in turn outputs a high to the enable pin of IC2 disabling it too. That means that only IC1 is enabled at the start of the count.

When pin 11 of IC1 goes high, it disables IC1 and at the same time that high is fed to pin 5 of IC4-a. Because both inputs to IC4-a are now high, it's output goes low and that in turn enables IC2. When the output at pin 11 of IC2 goes high, it's inverted by IC4-b and the resulting low enables IC3. The same low is applied to IC4-a causing it to change states (go high), thus disabling IC2. After nine more clock pulses the output of IC3 at pin 11 goes high applying that signal to all of the reset pins simultaneously, causing all the 4017's to reset to zero and start the whole sequence all over again.

Essentially, what we're doing is using pin 11 of each 4017 to control the enable pin of the next IC in line. When the output at pin 11 of the last IC in the sequence goes high, a high is applied to the reset pins of all the IC's causing them to be reset to the beginning. The same principle can be used to extend the sequence. Just remember that you can only use eight of the 4017's ten outputs—pin 3 is needed because there's no inhibit control and pin 11 controls the next 4017.

USING THE 4018

Anyone who spends a lot of time hacking around with hardware soon finds out that there are certain kinds of circuit requirements that pop up over and over again. Forget the old axiom that there is nothing new under the sun—it's only half right. There may only be a few new questions, but there are always lots of new answers. One of the words to keep your eyes peeled for when you're browsing through data books is "programmable." Whenever you see that word, pay special attention to what follows because there's a good chance that the information there can save you all sorts of trouble.

The 4018 is billed as a "programmable" counter, meaning that it can be preset to perform division by any number up to ten. And, like the 4017, it can be cascaded to increase the range of division; that is, two IC's will divide by 100, three by 1000, and so on. Now, those of you out there who have been following along on our little trip through the "suburbs of counterland" will probably be wondering why the 4017 was called a "decade counter" while the 4018 enjoys the added adjective of "programmable." Well, the answer is really simple.

When we used the 4017 for frequency division, there were lots of problems we had to overcome. Some of them, like fixing the reset, could be handled by adding a bunch of extra parts to the circuit. Other problems, like the duty cycle of the output, weren't quite that simple to handle. Squaring up the output of the 4017 for any kind of division would have required the kind of hardware design that went out the window with 200-watt soldering irons

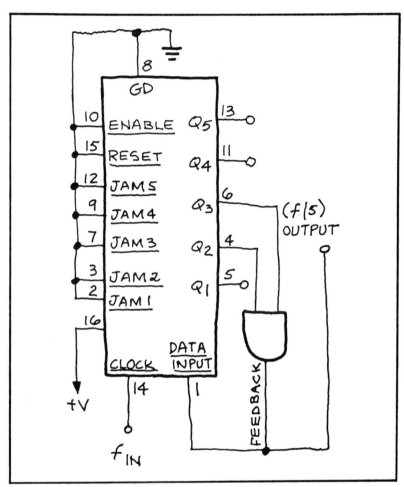

Fig. 6-2.

and 12-gauge wire. What we mean is that the 4017 wasn't really designed to handle the job of frequency division. Sure, if all you care about is knowing "how many" over a period of time, the IC will do the job. But if your application is finicky about the output waveform, you'll have to turn to the 4018. The 4018 is a real "divide-by-n counter" while the 4017 is simply called a "counter."

In order to explore that a bit further, let's make the 4018 do something and see how it differs from the 4017.

First of all, there are two ways we can use the 4018—let's call them the "fixed" and "preset" modes;

TABLE 6-1.

JAM1	JAM2	JAM3	JAM4	JAM5	COUNT	Q1	Q2	Q3	Q4	Q5
0	0	0	0	0	0	1	1	1	1	1
1	0	0	0	0	1	0	1	1	1	1
1	1	0	0	0	2	0	0	1	1	1
1	1	1	0	0	3	0	0	0	1	1
1	1	1	1	0	4	0	0	0	0	1
1	1	1	1	1	5	0	0	0	0	0
0	1	1	1	1	6	1	0	0	0	0
0	0	1	1	1	7	1	1	0	0	0
0	0	0	1	1	8	1	1	1	0	0
0	0	0	0	1	9	1	1	1	1	0

let's talk about the fixed mode first. In that mode, the IC can do pretty much what the 4017 did—divide by any number from 2 to 10. The device requires a feedback loop to operate and the output is picked off the feedback path at pin 1, the data input.

Figure 6-2 shows a typical circuit using the 4018. In that figure, the IC is set up in the fixed mode to perform frequency division by five. Since we're not using the preset features of the IC, we have to ground the JAM inputs as well as the RESET and ENABLE pins. That is standard practice for all unused CMOS inputs. Although the ENABLE pin really controls the preset functions of the IC, you can think of it as somewhat similar to the ENABLE pin of the 4017.

In any event, the proper feedback signal is provided by AND-ing the Q2 and Q3 outputs together and tying them back to the DATA input of the IC. Once we do that, the incoming frequency is fed into the clock input and, as we said, we can pick off the divided output from the feedback path.

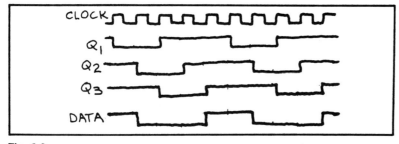

Fig. 6-3.

In order to appreciate the unique mess of the IC, take a look at Fig. 6-3. Those are the waveforms you would see if you looked at various points in the circuit using an oscilloscope. Take a really good look at them because .there's more here than is readily apparent—a little imagination will open up all sorts of wild possibilities.

Just as with the 4017, each of the Q outputs is phase-shifted from the previous one by exactly one (incoming) clock pulse. The difference lies in the fact that the unused outputs of the 4017 only stayed high for one clock pulse, causing the output waveforms to be really spike-filled and irregular. As you can see from the figure, the 4018 has an output frequency equal to the incoming clock frequency divided by whatever number we selected to divide by. The duty cycle is always "just about" fifty percent. We say "just about" because division by odd numbers is going to throw the output duty cycle "out of square" by exactly one period of the clock frequency. That is really only a minor annoyance and easy to live with—especially if you remember what the output waveforms of the 4017 looked like.

If we look at the output waveform in Fig. 6-3, we can see that things turned out as we could have predicted. Since we're AND-ing outputs Q2 and Q3 together, the output is high only when both Q2 and Q3 are high.

If you're dividing by ten, you can get the same output symmetry from the 4017 by taking the output from pin 12, the CARRY OUT pin. What's so special about the 4018 is that division by any number from two to ten will produce the same symmetry at the output. All that you have to do is feed the required Q outputs back to the DATA input. At most, the whole thing is going to cost you one AND gate, and that's a pretty cheap price to pay. If you don't have a spare gate on the board you can always accomplish the same things with a pair of diodes and a resistor, or some other similar arrangement.

PRESET MODE

Now let's see what happens in the preset mode—so we can use the programmable features of the 4018. The

JAM and ENABLE pins allow us to preset the 4018 to divide by any number we want. What's happening inside the IC is really very straightforward. Remember that what we are dealing with is nothing more than a series of interconnected flip-flops. The 4017 is a "serial-input-only" type of shift register while the 4018 has both serial and parallel inputs. When we use the 4018's JAM inputs, what we're really doing is presenting the appropriate information to the SET inputs of the internal flip-flops and then strobing that information into internal latches by taking pin 10, the ENABLE pin, briefly high.

A keyboard encoder uses the same sort of strobing technique to latch selected keyboard entry onto the data

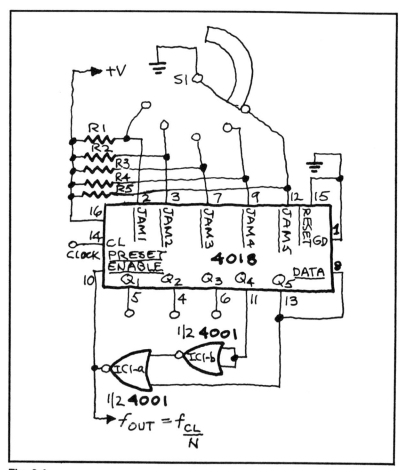

Fig. 6-4.

bus. What's happening here with the 4018 is exactly the same sort of thing. The designer of the IC was kind enough to put the latches on the substrate for us, so we don't have to go through the brain damage of hardwiring it ourselves. The code that we have to use to preset a number in the 4018 is, however, not a standard sort of code. That makes sense when we look at Fig. 6-6, a block diagram of the 4018's guts.

As you can see, what we have is a series of five flip-flops daisy-chained together. The incoming frequency of the clock line controls the speed at which the data is going to be routed through the flip-flops. The actual data is just various combinations of the Q outputs of the flip-flops that are fed back to the start of the daisy chain. If you think of that whole arrangement as a shift register, which is what it really is, you should have no trouble understanding exactly what's going on. Parallel loading with the JAM inputs is exactly the same as loading a shift register with parallel inputs. As a matter of fact, you should be able to see that the code that has to be used to load a number into the IC is the same code that the Q outputs present for any particular number.

When you reset the IC using the JAM inputs, all you're really doing is forcing the IC to start its count as if that number had already been reached by means of feeding the serial input. In other words, parallel loading a number is going to make the IC start its count at that number. Frequency division will have to be rethought a bit, since the IC is going to start out at a particular number and then reset to that same number when the count in the IC reaches 10. If you want to divide by four for instance, you'll have to load a six into the IC. That way the IC will reset after $10 - 6 = 4$ counts. That may sound confusing but five minutes of actually playing with the IC will make it clear.

Parallel loading should make you think about what you have to do to make the operation switch-selectable. A simple rotary switch (if you're lazy) or a keyboard select (if you're ambitious) should allow you to divide by any number you choose, and the IC will provide glitch-free, highly symmetrical outputs. The added advantage of using that IC over the 4017 is that the output will be square, (or nearly square), regardless of the shape of the incoming wave.

MORE ON THE 4018

Before we see what's necessary to make the 4018 start to do things in the real world, it's a good idea to spend a little time going over the circuitry we need to make the device programmable. The first thing you should realize if you start playing with the IC is that the JAM inputs and Q outputs are complimentary—when an input is low, the corresponding output is high. The reason for that apparent bit of insanity has to do with the internal design of the device and is just one of those things we'll have to live with. In passing, it should be mentioned that there are ways to take care of that if you regard it as a problem.

Remember that that IC is really a series of daisy-chained flip-flops: i.e., a shift register with parallel and serial inputs. When we make it programmable, all we're doing is preloading the flip-flops. That fact coupled with the fact that the zero count has all high on the outputs, makes the coding of the 4018 unique. Table 6-1 is a listing of the code to keep in mind when you use the JAM inputs.

In Fig. 6-4 resistors R1 and R5 hold all the JAM inputs high. They're selectively brought low with S1, a rotary switch that encodes all the inputs properly. The 4018 won't pay any attention to the JAM inputs unless the PRESET ENABLE pin, pin 10, is brought high. That is taken care of by IC1-a and IC1-b, half of a 4001 QUAD NOR gate. If you look at the data in Table 6-1 you'll see that Q4 and Q5 can be decoded when the count reaches nine and we can use that to flash a high at the PRESET ENABLE. If that looks strange compared to the 4017, remember that preloading the 4018 at the JAM inputs means that we're telling the IC what number to start the count with; on the 4017 we were telling the IC what number to end the count with. That may seem a bit strange but such are the peculiarities of things in the digital world. Seriously though, it's really a very important point and you should make sure you understand it.

There is a fundamental difference in the 4018's fixed and programmed modes. Obviously the hardware is different, but there's also a difference in just how the IC goes about actually dividing a frequency. In the fixed mode, the data on the selected output pins is constantly being recirculated through the internal flip-flops.

When the count reaches the number you've chosen for division, a logic one (high) is force-fed to the DATA input and appears at the $Q1$ output with the arrival of the next incoming clock pulse. What is really happening here is that a particular stream of ones and zeros are trapped in the IC. Division, then, is being done by starting with a count of zero and working our way up the ladder.

Fixed mode division, as we've already seen, is quite a different thing. We preload the beginning number and let the device count from there to ten. The output frequency in that case can be picked off the DATA input just as it was in the fixed mode, but the waveforms are very different in the two cases. With fixed-mode division we wind up with a 50/50, or nearly 50/50, duty cycle. In the programmed mode, symmetry is out the window.

What, you may very well ask, is the advantage in using that IC? Well, the parts count is lower in circuits using the 4018 than in circuits using the 4017—only two external gates are needed as opposed to four—and we have a means of programming the IC that is completely independent of the outputs. If you think about that for a moment and take another look at Fig. 6-2, you'll realize that the rotary switch there could easily be replaced by something much more exciting and versatile, namely a microprocessor.

A SINEWAVE GENERATOR

For the moment, however, let's get back to the reason we started playing around with the 4018. Look at the timing diagram in Fig. 6-3, the first thing that comes to mind is that the symmetry of the outputs is perfect for generating sinewaves. As a matter of fact, that is one of the most common uses for the 4018. Before we actually start doing the design, let's lay down the design criteria.

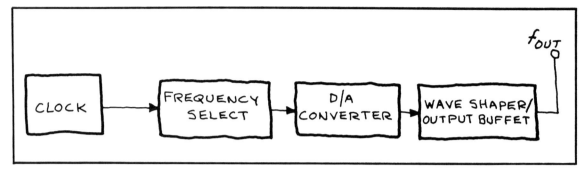

Fig. 6-5.

1. The parts count will be as low as possible.
2. Battery operation will be possible.
3. The bandwidth will be at least 100 Hz to 100 kHz.
4. The output frequency will be controlled by a potentiometer.

There are all sorts of additional bells and whistles that we could add to that list—readouts, keyboard frequency-selection, and so on. All those sorts of things are design problems on their own and are really beside the point. Once we've described the basics we can spend a bit of time exploring the extras.

If you stop and think about it for a moment, the basic method behind generating a sinewave with a 4018 is simple. Of course, that's just the basic method. Just as with anything in electronics, once you get past the beginning, things have a nasty habit of getting incredibly hairy. How sharp your razor has to be in order to cut through it all depends on a lot of things ranging from the depth of your interest to the extent of your need.

As you should all know by now, the first step in any design is to make sure you know what you want to do and then work out the bare bones of the problem on paper. You can't talk about components and circuitry unless and until you've got a clear idea of your objectives and a block diagram of a possible solution in front of you. Since we know what we want to do, our next step is to draw a block diagram.

Figure 6-5 is a representation of what we want to design. It looks simple because the problem is simple—don't forget that we've already decided, at least for the moment, to drop a lot of the bells and whistles.

All of our discussions have been aimed at laying the groundwork for an understanding of the design of the D/A converter shown in the block diagram. All we're talking about there is using the 4018 to convert a stream of clock pulses into something that can be made into a sinewave. How we would go about doing that should be evident after a quick look at the 4018 timing chart in Fig. 6-3. All that wonderful regularity at the outputs is just perfect for what we have in mind. It's a matter of adding the outputs together in some way to create an up and down staircase that we can iron smooth with the wave shaper.

As with any D/A conversion, the more digital steps you start with, the better the analog signal you wind up with. Since the 4018 has five internal flip-flops, we'll use them all. Not only will that give us the maximum number

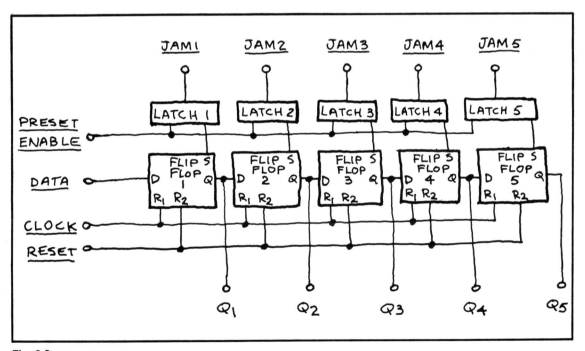

Fig. 6-6.

of digital steps, but it helps us satisfy the first of our design criteria—keeping the parts count down. Using all the flip-flops in the device means that we're setting it up to divide by ten. Again, take a look at Fig. 6-3 if you're not clear about that. When you use the 4018 for fixed division by ten, the external parts count is exactly zero! You can't do much better than that.

If the IC is going to be dividing by ten, it follows logically that the input clock has to run ten times faster than the maximum frequency we want for our sinewave. Criterion 3 means that we're going to need an input clock that can put out everything from a minimum of 1 kHz to a top of at least 1 MHz.

Section 7: USING THE 4089 AND 5101 MICROPROCESSOR

THIS SECTION BRIEFLY DETAILS SOME OF THE USES FOR THE 4089 rate multiplier and the low-power 5101 CMOS IC's.

COUNTING WITH THE 4089

I'm a real freak when it comes to paperwork, data sheets, and generally anything that makes life on the bench a little easier. That's because it's always a good idea to collect as much information as possible before you start "getting your hands dirty."

However, there are limits to how much information you can absorb. Sooner or later you'll find it impossible to learn any more from paperwork alone. That means that you must actually work with a device in order to truly understand its operation. So, in line with that sage advice, let's get our hands dirty, and see what we must do with rate multipliers to make them perform some useful task.

USING RATE MULTIPLIERS

We'll be using the 4089 for our discussion because

in the first place, it's a CMOS IC—I believe in using CMOS whenever possible. Second, I just happen to have some of them lying around the house—always an important consideration when trying to cut costs!

Although the numbers may seem confusing at first, you'll find that actually powering up one of these IC's will make its use a lot clearer. As with most other special-purpose IC's, the majority of the control pins are held either high or low during normal operation. That greatly simplifies understanding how the IC works.

The majority of uses for the rate multiplier will revolve around some sort of arithmetic—usually multiplication or division. Other kinds of operations are possible as well (because more-complex arithmetic, such as square roots or exponential functions, can usually be reduced to repetitive basic arithmetic). But, let's start off by seeing what we have to do to multiply two numbers together.

MULTIPLICATION CIRCUIT

Figure 7-1 is a block diagram of the circuit we want to put together to multiply "X" times "Y." Although there are a number of boxes there, things aren't as complicated as they may seem to be. The basic operation of the circuit is simple and the clock can be any type of arrangement that you want to use, as long as it's noise-free and the waveforms look something like a squarewave.

A basic 555 oscillator or some other type of clocking arrangement works fine. You may be wondering about the frequency needed from the clock. Well, the answer to that question will surprise you: It doesn't matter what the frequency is! How's that for simplicity? But right now, let's clean off our hands and see why that apparently screwball statement is true.

First consider how the rate multiplier works: It takes the input-clock frequency, does some internal division and gives us two kinds of outputs.

Now recall that the "base-rate" is equal to one sixteenth the input clock, and that the "multiplied-rate" is the base rate multiplied by whatever number is

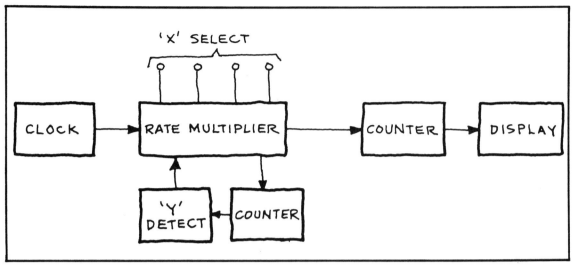

Fig. 7-1.

presented at the binary inputs. If we were to write that statement as a formula, it would look something like this:

Base rate = Input Clock/16
Multiplied Rate = (X) (Input Clock/16)

Where "X" is one of the numbers we're multiplying.

That means that every time a pulse appears at the base-rate output, we'll get "X" number of pulses at the multiplied-rate output. To multiply "X" and "Y" all we need to do is count the base-rate pulses and stop after "Y" number of (multiplied-rate) pulses. Getting the right answer is really as simple as counting the total number of pulses at the multiplied-rate output, or expressed as a formula:

$$\text{Base Rate} = \text{Input Clock/16}$$
$$\text{Multiplied Rate} = (X) \ (\text{Base Rate})$$
$$= (X) \ (\text{Input Clock/16})$$

$$X = (\text{Multiplied Rate})/(\text{Base Rate})$$
$$X = \frac{[(X) \ (\text{Input Clock/16})}{(\text{Input Clock/16})]}$$

$$X = X$$

As you can see, when we're doing multiplication with a rate multiplier, both the input clock and the internal base-number of the IC are completely unimportant—they cancel out. Getting the answer is only a matter of, as we said before, keeping track of the base-rate output pulses and counting up the multiplied-rate pulses.

The only part of Fig. 7-1 that could be at all tricky is the counter and other associated circuitry needed to detect when "Y" number of pulses have been generated at the base-rate output. There are two ways to do that. The method that you choose depends mostly on the type of counter you decide to use.

Since we want to count something "Y" times, we can either use an up counter starting at zero to detect "Y," or preload a down counter with "Y" to detect a zero. The choice again depends on the IC you want to use. Because up counters are a lot easier to come by, that's the way we'll go. Just remember that it's only a matter of personal choice.

One of the nicest things about CMOS counters is that there's a whole range of ripple counters that provide a one-IC solution to problems just like ours. They come in really handy when you want to count to some large number.

The 4020, 4040, and 4060 are all members of the ripple-counter family, but of those only the 4040 has outputs covering a continuous 12-stage count. That means that you can use it to detect any number from 0 to 4096.

Figure 7-2 shows the pinout of the 4040. It's used just the way you'd expect it to be; a clock is routed to pin 10, the reset pin is held low, and the IC will advance one count on the negative-going edge of each incoming clock pulse.

Detecting "Y" involves a bit of gating. How you set things up, naturally, depends on the number that you're trying to detect. For instance, let's say that we want to multiply 14 by 67.

The only special thing about picking the numbers to be multiplied is to make sure that one of them is less

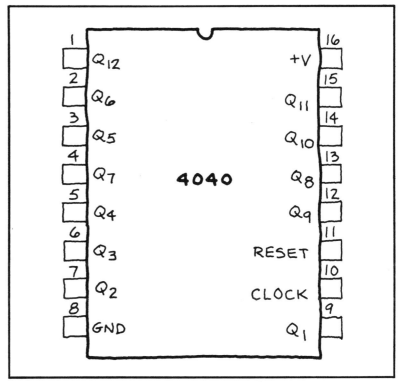

Fig. 7-2.

than 16. That's because the 4089 has only four weighted inputs and the highest number that those inputs can represent is 15 (or 1111 in binary). However, the 4089 is easily cascaded for larger numbers. We'll examine that in more detail once we get through our example.

Figure 7-3 is a schematic of the circuit that we're designing; it shows everything except the counter and the display. We'll deal with them later.

The weighted inputs of the 4089 are set to load in a binary 14 (1110). We'll be using ⅓ of a 4073, 3-input AND gate to decode the Q1, Q2, and Q7 outputs of the 4040. Switch S1 is used to start the whole business going.

When S1 is pressed, IC3 resets and causes the output of the IC4-a to go low. That enables the rate multiplier, IC2, by bringing pin 11 low, causing it to start sending base-rate pulses to the clock input of IC3. For each base-rate pulse, 14 pulses are output at pin 6, the MULTIPLIED-RATE OUTPUT. You can see that the way we're doing our

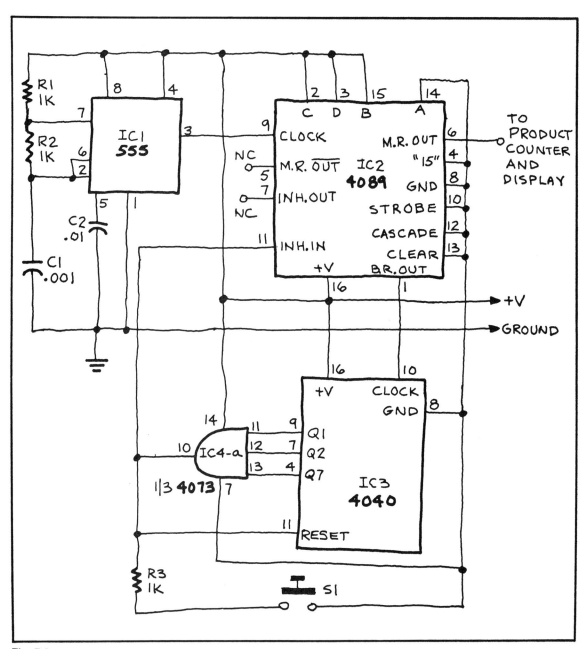

Fig. 7-3.

multiplication is to make IC2 count to 14 over and over
until it's done it 67 times.

When that happens, 67 is decoded and the output
of IC4-a goes high. That resets IC3 to zero and brings the

INHIBIT INPUT (pin 11) of IC2 high, preventing it from putting out any more pulses.

You could easily modify the circuit and use a gated oscillator so that the 4073 (IC4-a) would also stop the clock—there are many ways to accomplish that.

Since IC3 is reset to zero each time the circuit is used, any number that comes after 67 will never appear at the output. If you use a number other than 67, (which you probably will), you'll more than likely have to use a gate with more input legs. Not to worry though, because that can be taken care of by the two remaining gates in the 4073.

To add more inputs, just use a second gate as an input device and the third one to AND the first two together. It's not too difficult to figure out what gating you have to use.

MAKING THE 4089 DO USEFUL THINGS

One of the nicest things about designing logic circuits is that they're, well, so logical. All you need do is figure out what you want the circuit to do, work out a flow chart or block diagram of the unit, find the parts, and that's that.

Well, to be truthful about it, there's a bit more to it than that (as we all know), but the creative work can all be done on paper. Once the circuit has been breadboarded, there are always certain minor technical problems to be taken care of—like the unit doesn't work. But that's circuit *hacking*, not circuit *design*.

Anybody who's been following our discussion on rate multipliers and has breadboarded the circuit, we worked out last time, should've found the 4089 to be really simple to use.

In our last discussion of rate multipliers, we left out part of the circuit—the display—because, as previously stated, you can use any counter arrangement that you're familiar with. All you need is a circuit that's able to count and display the number of digits you expect to see in your answer.

We'll add the display circuitry and also take a look

at what must be done to make our circuit do useful things. We'll begin our discussion with the display circuit.

THE DISPLAY

Before we get into our discussion, here's a little advice that can save you plenty of trouble in the long run. One of the best habits to get into when designing is to keep a notebook containing schematics of often-used circuits. Remember Grossblatt's 15th law: *Never trust your memory!*

A counter-display combination is used almost as often as a clock circuit and, therefore, is a natural addition to your files. With that out of the way, let's get to it!

In the example we used for the circuit last time around, we were multiplying 14 times 67. That means we'll need 3 digits (to display 938). Since we'll be counting three digits and using CMOS logic, the 4553 decade counter/multiplexer is a good choice. We will couple it to a standard 4511 decoder driver.

Figure 7-4 shows the pinouts for both those IC's. You should be familiar with the 4511 (Fig. 7-4) used to drive the displays in the keyboard encoder. It's a "plain vanilla" decoder/driver for common-cathode displays.

The 4553 (Fig. 7-4B) is a mainstream device that has all the circuitry needed to count up to 999 on board, as well as the multiplexing logic to directly handle three digits. The IC also contains three cascaded synchronous-counters whose outputs time-share pins 5, 6, 7, and 9.

The individual digits are turned on by using the three DISPLAY-ENABLE pins (1, 2, and 15). The RESET, LATCH-ENABLE, and CHIP-ENABLE pins are self explanatory (they're the same as similar controls found on other IC's). Pins 3 and 4 are the external-world connections for the timing capacitor used by the on-board, low-frequency multiplexing oscillator.

Although you may find the 4553 a bit on the expensive side—usually about three or four dollars by mail order—it's a good choice because it takes the place of a whole handful of IC's. The savings in board complexity, power consumption, and bench time make

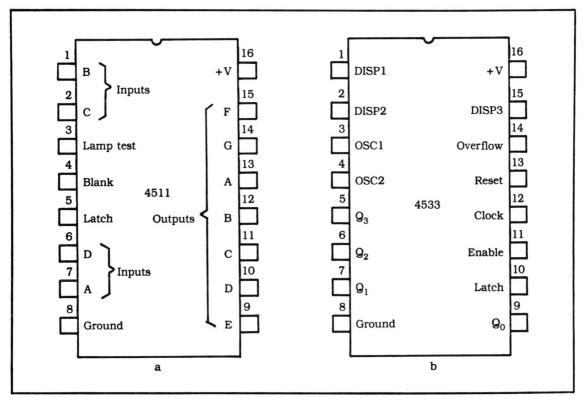

Fig. 7-4.

it more than worth the extra cost.

Figure 7-5 is the schematic for the display portion of the rate-multiplier demonstration circuit. Because the parts count is low, designing a printed circuit board for it is a snap. (You should be able to fit everything on a small, single-sided board.)

By coupling the circuit in Fig. 7-5 to the one we worked out already for the 4089, you'll have yourself a complete demonstrator for a rate multiplier. Admittedly, the circuit isn't the most useful circuit in the world, since it's hard-wired to multiply two particular numbers together. But we'll talk about how to make it a little more versatile in a little bit.

We've already seen how easy it is to do multiplication, but what about division? Well, believe it or not, adapting our circuit to do division is simple. But first, let's go through a quick run down on the theory behind doing multiplication. The rate multiplier takes an

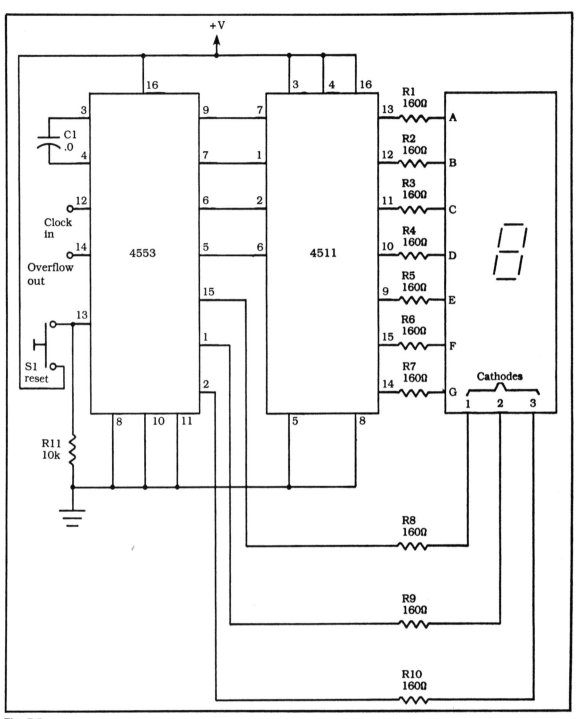

Fig. 7-5.

input clock and gives us two different kinds of outputs—the base rate and the multiplied rate.

The relation between the two is controlled by a 4-bit word (number) presented to the IC's data or weighted inputs. The multiplied rate will be equal to the product of the base rate and the binary word. As mentioned in previous discussions, doing multiplication is really just successive addition. We keep track of the base-rate pulses and count the multiplied-rate pulses.

MORE ON THE 4089

This time, let's start off by seeing how the 4089 can be used to do division.

DIVISION WITH RATE MULTIPLIERS

Since we treated multiplication as successive addition, let's think of division as successive subtraction. In simpler terms, how many times can we subtract one number from another before we reach zero? To be practical about it, let's take a look at the circuit from our last discussion.

What we want to do with the circuit this time around is to keep track of the multiplied-rate pulses and count the base-rate pulses (the opposite of what we did previously). In hardware terms, that means we have to switch two wires in the circuit!

Figure 7-6 can be considered an addendum to the circuit we did; it shows the extra hardware needed to switch between the multiplication and division modes. With the display added, all we need do is put a DPDT switch to change the operation of the circuit from multiplication to division.

Doing more complex forms of arithmetic, such as square and roots, is possible as well. Virtually any arithmetic operation can be written as a series of operations that involve only multiplication and division. A good mathematics textbook will show you what has to be done.

Once you have that taken care of, arrange your circuit to do the necessary arithmetic and that should be

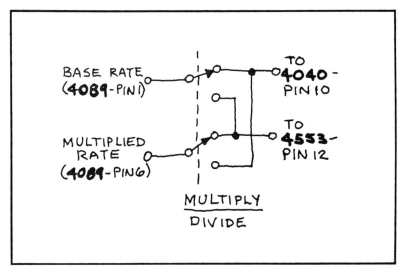

Fig. 7-6.

that. Start out with square roots and continue from there.

There are two problems left for us to talk about. The first is figuring out a way to make the circuit easier to use and the second is making the circuit more useful. Let's tackle the second one first.

CASCADING THE 4089

The 4089, and all the other rate multipliers, are easy to cascade and there are two different ways of doing it. Which way you choose depends on the kind of arithmetic you want to do.

In Fig. 7-7A, the IC's are cascaded in what National Semiconductor calls the "add" mode. IC1 works just the way it did in our demonstrator circuit and if you were to check the output of IC1, you would see the same results we saw earlier. Things aren't terribly straightforward when you're in the "add" mode, however. Since IC2 has its cascade input connected to the output of IC1, its multiplied rate will be 16 times greater than that of IC1.

On the other hand, if you wanted to do division—let's say, 72—you would have to remember that IC1 is working with a base of 16 and IC2 is working with a base of 256 (16 times 16). In order to figure out what numbers to present to the inputs of the 4089, you have to do some additional work to reduce everything to a base of 256.

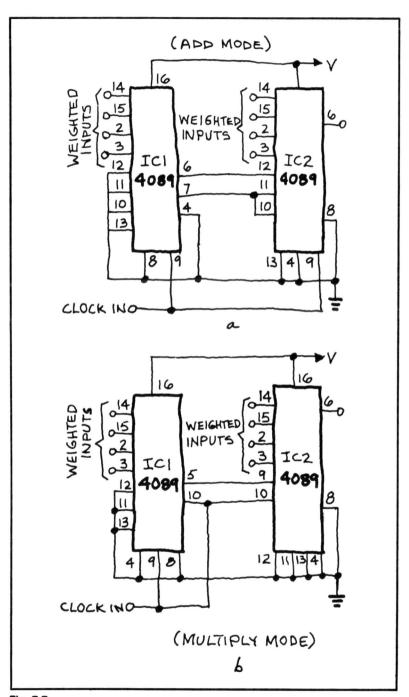

Fig. 7-7.

If A is the most significant digit (at IC1) and B is the least significant digit (at IC2) then:

$$(A \times 16) + B = 72$$

The trick is to find how large you can make A without exceeding 73. Minor brain burning gives us an answer of four for A; therefore, B has to be eight. To sum it up, we put a binary four (0100) and a binary eight (1000) at the weighted inputs of rate multipliers IC1 and IC2, respectively.

A much easier way to take care of that is to use the second method of cascading the 4089, which National Semiconductor refers to as the "multiply" mode. That configuration, shown in Fig. 7-7B, is a standard cascading arrangement. It is more common than the "add" mode, but as we'll soon see, it is not as versatile.

The procedure is a little different and a lot simpler than the previous method. Here the outputs of the IC's are multiplied together in a normal cascade arrangement, making the arithmetic a lot easier, as can be seen from the equation:

$$A \times B = 72$$

Our only restriction in choosing values for A and B is the four-bit width of the IC's; 12 and 6 are the only choices.

You've probably noticed that not all numbers can be obtained using that method, which is why the add mode is more versatile. However, if we were doing multiplication, the restriction wouldn't apply and this method would be better, since it would mean fewer traces on the board.

Like almost everything else in digital circuitry, our description makes it sound much more complicated than it really is. If you try working with the rate multiplier, you'll find that it can provide easy solutions to what would otherwise be seemingly impossible circuit problems.

PUTTING THE 5101 TO WORK

There's a kind of natural law governing the development of new electronic equipment. As the revision numbers on the boards go up, the amount of power drawn by the unit goes down. Something that starts life needing 86 percent of the output of the TVA usually winds up, a couple of revisions later, one tenth the size and running on barometric pressure!

Much of that progress is due to more efficient design, custom IC's, and microprocessors. But the major factor is the continuing evolution of CMOS technology.

The 5101 was an early entry into the low-power CMOS market. When it first appeared, most designers were knocked out of their socks by its low-power characteristics, and its guarantee to retain data at a low-power figure. Although technology has gone beyond the 5101, knowing how to use its low-power feature is still important.

MEMORY CONTROL

Although the data sheet for the 5101 gives the impression that using its standby feature is as easy as putting the right voltage on pin 17, there's a bit more to it than that. To be sure that your data doesn't disappear in the standby mode, there are four hard-and-fast rules that must be followed closely and in a certain order:

- The IC has to be locked in the read mode.
- The address lines have to be stabilized.
- All inputs and outputs must be turned off.
- The transition to standby power has to be glitch-free.

Locking the IC in the read mode is important, but often overlooked. Remember that you can write to the 5101 when R/$\overline{\text{W}}$ is brought low. That line is also brought low when system power is disconnected. But if another line stays active for any time after that, a phony-baloney write is generated. That means that the next time the circuit is powered up, you'll find some of the data overwritten.

There are two ways we can guard against that. One way is to lock the operation of pin 19, CHIP ENABLE, to the power-down procedure. The other way is to directly control the R/W̄ pin, and synchronize it to the transition to standby.

CONTROL SYNCHRONIZATION

If you lock the device in read by directly controlling the R/W̄ pin, the address lines must remain unchanged. However, the more traditional way is to completely disable the IC. Then what's going on with the address bus is irrelevant.

The same thing applies to the I/O. Disabling the entire IC, naturally, disconnects the IC from the I/O bus. However, if things are done differently, you'll have to design a circuit that first disconnects the memory from system I/O. The outputs are no problem since the 5101 has a separate control (pin 18) to three-state the output. But a buffer arrangement of some type is needed for the inputs.

The last rule, and the last operation to be done, is to make sure that the switch-over to standby is completely glitch-free. No matter how well you design the rest of the procedure, if there's much bouncing at the +V pin at shutdown, you're sure to foul up the data stored in the memory.

Now that we have an idea of what must be done to use the standby feature of the IC, let's put it to practical use in the circuit we've been designing. The best way to set things up is to lock the operation of the STANDBY control, pin 17, to the CHIP ENABLE, pin 19, if we do that and sync them properly, as shown in Fig. 7-8, we'll be sure that the IC is put to sleep properly, and that the timing is correct. You'll note that an automatic backup battery supply is shown separated from the rest of the circuit by dashed lines. It simply kicks in automatically when there is a power failure.

Note also that pin 17 and pin 19 are controlled by the same line on the data bus and are separated from each

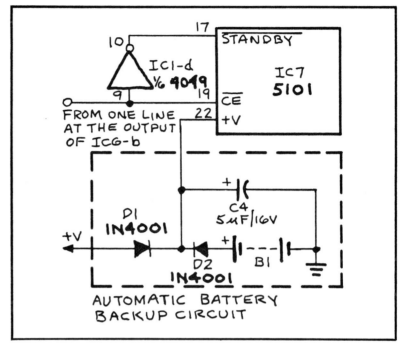

Fig. 7-8.

other by a spare inverter. If you look over the truth table of the 5101 you'll see exactly what's going on.

As long as the line feeding the memory is kept low, the entire IC is enabled. That low also causes the inverter to output a high to pin 17, taking the IC out of the standby mode. A low sensed at pin 17 puts the IC to sleep. But that inverter does more than let us lock the operation of both control pins together.

Remember that we're concerned with both the state of those pins, and the order in which things happen. If we don't sync things properly, the IC will go to sleep, but the data will probably glitch. The propagation delay of the inverter makes sure that that part of the power down operation happens in the right order.

When a high is applied to pin 19, the entire IC is disabled. And later, after a propagation delay, the standby mode is chosen. That means we have to modify the schematic of the circuit we've been building. By tying the operation of pins 17 and 19 together, we need only three of the lines coming out of IC6-b.

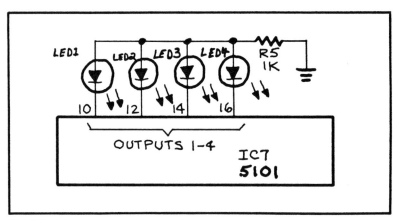

Fig. 7-9.

The last thing to consider in our demonstration circuit is what to do about the display. Unfortunately, standard display drivers are going to be somewhat inadequate. Unless you use oddball IC's, display drivers do really weird things when presented with straight binary data. Everything is fine as long as you stick to BCD. But if the most-significant bit is high, the display will usually be useless.

For our purposes, the easiest thing to do (as Fig. 7-9 shows) is to just hang LED's off the outputs. You can do the same thing on the outputs of the latches. That gives you a way to see what's happening on the address and data bus while keeping an eye on the state of the memory's control pins. (I'm the first to admit that that's a less-than-ideal solution.)

Getting standard display drivers like the 4511 or 7448 to deliver meaningful information when presented with straight binary is a tricky business.

Section 8: USING THE Z80 MICROPROCESSOR

Before beginning our journey into microprocessor land, you must have a road map. The only way you're going to get anything out of our discussion is to have a good Z80 databook in front of you.

CONTROL SIGNALS OF THE Z80 MICROPROCESSOR

The registers are the easiest part of the IC to understand. After all, they're nothing more than simple memory, similar to the RAM (*Random Access Memory*) we spent so much time talking about. What's unique about the registers is that they are located inside the Z80 itself. There are basically two kinds of registers: those that can only be accessed by the Z80, and those that are accessible to us.

The Z80, like any other microprocessor, spends its time following the instructions we give it. It uses certain registers to keep track of what it's doing, where it's going, and to store interim data. The other registers—the ones accessible to us—are pretty much the same as other memory you might interface to the microprocessor. The

main difference is that they're part of the IC itself, **and**
that provides two advantages over external memory.
First, the Z80 can get to the registers quicker than to
external memory, and second, it leaves the external data
bus free for use by other devices while the Z80 is busy
internally.

THE Z80

Figure 8-1 shows a pinout of the Z80. I've grouped
the pins by function in order to show relationships be-

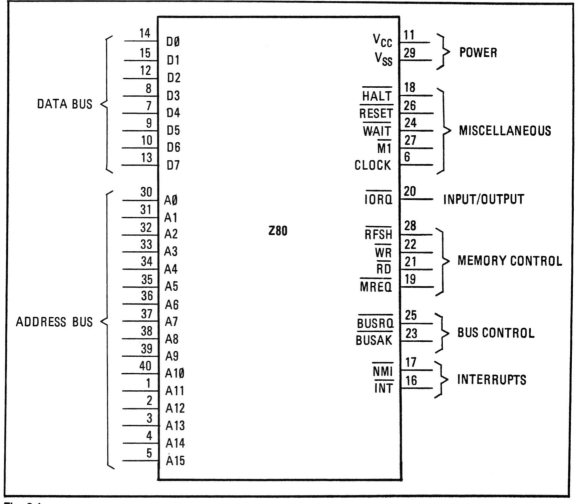

Fig. 8-1.

tween various groups of signals. The data and address buses are shown along the left side of the diagram, and the control signals along the right side.

The width of the address bus (i.e., the number of address lines) limits the number of external memory locations the Z80 can reference without resorting to special tricks. Since there is a total of 16 lines, the IC can directly access 2^{16}, or 65,536 locations.

The operation of the address and data bus controllers, and the ALU, are all affected by the state of pins 16 to 28. So let's take a look at them now.

BUS CONTROL SIGNALS

Typically, a microprocessor-based system will have several different devices interfaced to its address and data buses at any one time. But since only one device at a time can have control of those buses, the microprocessor needs to be informed when another device wants control. That task is taken care of by the $\overline{\text{BUSRQ}}$ (*BUS ReQuest*) input. A device that needs control of the bus sends a low to that pin. When that signal is received by the Z80, two things happen in sequence. First, both buses are tri-stated (placed at a high impedance) so that other devices can access them. Second, the Z80 lets all the interfaced devices know that the buses are available by placing a low on the $\overline{\text{BUSAK}}$ (*BUS AcKnowledge*) output. The buses stay tristated as long as there is a low on the $\overline{\text{BUSRQ}}$ input.

MEMORY-CONTROL SIGNALS

The most complex signals on the Z80 are those controlling external memory. Whenever the Z80 wants to access that memory, it puts a low on pin 19, the $\overline{\text{MREQ}}$ (*Memory REQuest*) line. That signal tells the rest of the circuit to release the data and address buses because the CPU wants to do something with external memory. Whether it's a read or a write depends on the signals found on pin 21 and 22, the $\overline{\text{RD}}$ (*ReaD*) and $\overline{\text{WR}}$ (*WRite*) signals.

When the Z80 wants to read the contents of a

particular memory location, it puts lows on the $\overline{\text{MREQ}}$ and $\overline{\text{RD}}$ lines. That informs the rest of the circuit that the CPU is going to do a read. Likewise, it should come as no great surprise to learn that when the Z80 wants to do a write, it puts lows on the $\overline{\text{MREQ}}$ and $\overline{\text{WR}}$ lines. Of course, the Z80 reads and writes data only after giving the address bus time to stabilize.

$\overline{\text{MREQ}}$ is similar to signals we've generated in circuits that we've designed in previous columns. In both the keyboard encoder and the memory-demonstrator we generated signals that were used to enable various circuit elements at different times. Well, $\overline{\text{MREQ}}$ is just such a signal. When you dissect Z80 circuits, you'll always find that the $\overline{\text{MREQ}}$ line is tied, either directly or through some other circuitry, to the enable lines of external memory. Once the memory is enabled, the $\overline{\text{RD}}$ of $\overline{\text{WR}}$ lines is used to prepare memory for a read or write.

The last line associated with memory is the $\overline{\text{RFSH}}$ (*ReFreSH*) line at pin 28. When we were discussing dynamic RAM, I told you that even though refresh can be a pain in the neck, there are LSI IC's that ease a great deal of that pain. Well, the Z80 also has built-in circuitry that makes the job easier.

In order to refresh most dynamic RAM, you can periodically read the contents of each cell out and write it back in. However, there's a simpler way; as you'll remember from previous discussions, reading any one memory cell causes all cells in the entire row to be refreshed. Also, a row can be refreshed by simply addressing one of the cells in the row. So the refresh hassle would be simpler if we had a circuit that would increment an address counter. We would use that counter to address successive rows in the memory array automatically. And that's exactly what the Z80's *R* register does for us.

In order to understand how it works, let's digress for a moment and talk about how the Z80 processes the instructions you give it in a program. The first thing the Z80 does as it prepares for each new instruction is to fetch that instruction from memory. After the instruction has been fetched, the CPU spends some time decoding the instruction, and the outcome of that determines what the CPU will do next. So immediately after every instruction-fetch, the Z80 is busy internally and has no need for the address and data buses.

Once the instruction fetch is complete, the Z80 does four things in sequence. First it increments the R register, and then it places the contents of that register on the lower seven bits of the address bus. Next, it brings the $\overline{\text{MREQ}}$ and $\overline{\text{RFSH}}$ lines low. At that point the contents of the R register have stabilized, and may be used by external circuitry. Then it's up to that circuitry to use those signals to refresh dynamic RAM.

OTHER CONTROL SIGNALS

Of the control signals left, the only one that really interests us at the moment is $\overline{\text{RESET}}$. Undoubtedly you've seen that kind of signal before. With the Z80, bringing that pin low causes all bus and control lines to go into a high-impedance state; further, the program counter and R register are set to zero, and, in general, the CPU is brought to a very-well-defined state so that the software will be able to build on that.

THE WORLD'S SIMPLEST Z80 CIRCUIT

We've had theory up to our ears by now, so let's do something practical. You'll recall, I said that we were going to build the world's simplest Z80 system. Well, let's see how simple such a system can be.

No matter what you want to do with a Z80, the first thing you must take account of is the system clock. Considering how powerful the Z80 actually is, it's surprisingly unfussy about its clock. The main requirement is that the clock be TTL level; the frequency of oscillation depends on which Z80 you'll use. The plain-vanilla Z80 has a maximum operating frequency of 2.5 MHz, but other versions of the IC, those with "A" and "B" suffixes, will run at maximum speeds of 4 and 6 MHz, respectively.

We don't need to run our circuit that fast; and, in order to keep the peripheral circuitry simple—and save a couple of bucks in the process—we'll use a plain Z80 with a 1-MHz clock. Other requirements of the clock (such as rise time and duty cycle) are easy to handle. As a matter of fact, if you have a TTL-level squarewave with a duty cycle of 50 percent, you can pretty much ignore those restrictions altogether. And since the Z80's clock input appears as one TTL load, we can even drive it with a CMOS astable multivibrator.

The complete schematic for our Z80 circuit is shown in Fig. 8-2. The clock circuit shown there should look familiar. That's right; it's our handy-dandy, all-purpose CMOS clock circuit. You should be able to put one of those together in your sleep by now. The output frequency of that circuit is approximately equal to $1/(2.2 \times R2 \times C1)$, so the values shown should give us about 1 MHz. The additional gate is a buffer used to isolate the clock circuit from the Z80's clock input, because it needs a 330 ohm pullup resistor.

Believe it or not, the only other control signal we have to generate for our bare-bones system is RESET. You'll notice in Fig. 8-2 that I generate that signal with R3 and C2. They take care of power-up reset; if you want to be able to generate RESET manually as well, all you need do is wire a momentary switch in parallel with C2.

Now that we've got a clock and a reset pulse, the next thing to talk about is memory. There has to be a place to store the software that drives the circuit, so we have to add some ROM. I chose a 2716 EPROM because, of all the permanent memory around, EPROM's are about the easiest to program, and 2716's are both cheap and available. Connecting the EPROM to the Z80 is simple. The address pins on the EPROM go to corresponding pins on the microprocessor; likewise with the data pins.

The only part of the memory circuit that needs to be explained is the 2716's chip-enable pins. You'll recall from our earlier discussions that when the Z80 wants to read something from memory, it puts a low on both the $\overline{\text{MREQ}}$ and $\overline{\text{RD}}$ lines. Those lines are connected to the enable pins of the 2716 so that a read request from the

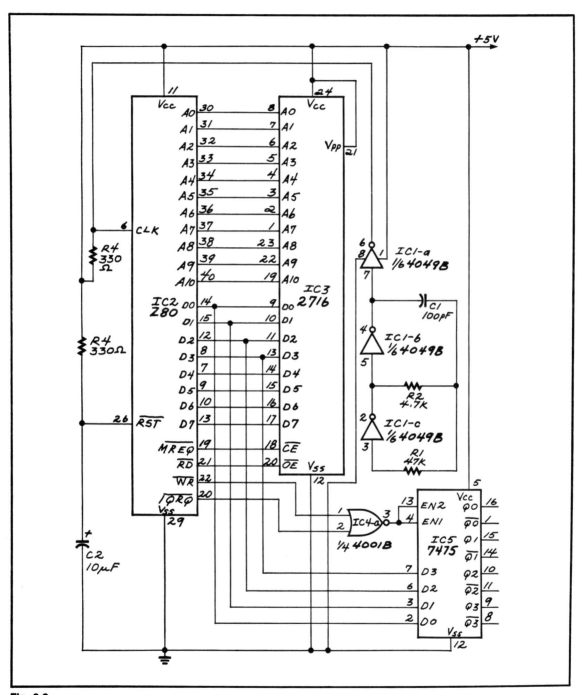

Fig. 8-2.

Z80 will enable the EPROM, thereby allowing data to be routed to the Z80.

So what about I/O? Well, in order to be consistent with our design goal of making this the world's simplest Z80 circuit, we'll connect a 7475 quad latch to the data bus. Whenever the Z80 wants to do an I/O operation, it puts a low on the $\overline{\text{IORQ}}$ line. The Z80 also brings $\overline{\text{WR}}$ or $\overline{\text{RD}}$ low depending on whether it wants to read from or write to an I/O port. So, by NOR'ing the $\overline{\text{IORQ}}$ and $\overline{\text{WR}}$ lines from the Z80, we can send data to the latch by using an OUT instruction. Since the enable pin of the 7475 is active high, the Z80 will be able to store data in the latch.

If you've been following my earlier columns on the Z80, there should be one question uppermost in your mind: What about the RAM?

WHERE'S THE RAM?

Even a minimal Z80 system needs some temporary storage space. There is such space, of course: the Z80's internal registers. There's not much space, but a system like ours doesn't really need much. We can run simple programs without any additional RAM storage.

So there we have a complete Z80 system with a minimum of components. In fact, there are more parts in some light dimmers! With our circuit the Z80 can read data and program instructions from the EPROM; it can also output data to the real world through the 4-bit latch. Actually, our little circuit can do quite a few things such as playing music, storing and displaying tables of data, or working as a simple controller. All you have to do is tell it what you want it to do. And there, as Shakespeare said, is the rub: software.

In order to deal with software you need a good grounding in both logic and the Z80's instruction set. The point is that microprocessor circuits, unlike the circuits we usually talk about, require very little understanding of electronics *per se*. Volts, ohms, amps, and all the rest go out the window.

SOFTWARE DOESN'T SMOKE!

I know it can be disconcerting for hardware hackers to come to grips with the fundamentals of Z80 circuit design. The fact of the matter is that the hardware represents at *most* only about 50 percent of the work required of any microprocessor circuit design.

If you hooked up the circuit, the experience probably turned out to be an exercise in unqualified frustration. You got the parts, connected them together—and absolutely nothing happened! The reason is simply that even though microprocessor-based circuits are very powerful, they're also very stupid. They can do anything you want them to do, but they can't do anything at all without very explicit instructions from you.

I'm sure you know I'm talking about software. That is a *big* subject, and there's simply no way we can cover it here in any depth. The best I can do is point out a few fundamentals, and try to steer you in the right direction to get more information.

We've mentioned the *instruction set* here before; it is simply the set of commands recognized by the microprocessor. Each instruction is passed from memory through the INSTRUCTION DECODER, and then carried out by the arithmetic logic unit (or ALU for short). All Z80 circuits must have space to store those commands; in the circuit we used an EPROM, although it could have been some other kind of memory.

THE HEX PROBLEM

Since we'll be dealing with the Z80 in low-level machine language (as opposed to BASIC or Pascal, which are high-level languages), there's one thing you'll have to come to grips with right away: dealing with hexadecimal numbers.

Instructions are presented to the Z80 on its eight-bit data bus in binary (that is, as ones and zeros), but straight binary is too difficult to deal with, so designers almost universally use hex. For example, the code for a JUMP instruction (similar to a GOTO in BASIC), is 11000011 to the Z80, but to human beings, it's C3.

If you're serious about using microprocessors, you've got to get to the point where you can look at a hex number and have a good intuitive feel for what it means. I know that's a pain in the neck, but it's easier than constantly converting to and from decimal numbers.

Both data and instructions are specified in hex. The Z80 has 158 basic instructions, but if you count all the different addressing modes, the actual number of instructions is almost three times as many. Since a byte (8 bits) can have only 256 different values, and since there are over 400 different instructions, some instructions must be more than one byte long. In fact, some instructions are four bytes long. Anyway, in order to give you a basic idea of the Z80's instruction set, I've grouped all the instructions in four categories, as shown in Table 8-1.

The first group of instructions in Table 8-1 has the most members. Those instructions include the LOAD series used to move data to and from external memory, the Z80's internal registers, and the I/O (input/output) devices connected to your system. Whenever you use one of these instructions, you have to supply two pieces of information:

1. The source of the data (i.e., which register or

TABLE 8-1. Z80 INSTRUCTION TYPES.

Function	Instructions	Descriptions
Data Movement	LD EX EXX IN OUT	This family moves data to and from CPU, memory, and I/O.
Data Changing	BIT SET RES ADD SUB AND OR XOR S R CP INC DEC	This is the largest series of instructions. They alter the data by doing arithmetic, bit level, and logical functions.
Program Flow	JP CALL RET	These can change in sequence of instructions in a program.
CPU Control	DI EI IMO IM1 IM2 HALT NOP	These let the Z-80 respond to events that aren't checked by the program being executed.

memory location), or the data itself.
2. The destination of the data.

There are 134 different data-movement instructions. Some of that variety is due to the fact that the Z80 has two main sets of register. The alternate B′C′ pair corresponds to the BC pair, D′E′ to DE, H′L′ to HL, and A′F′ to AF. Now, even though it's correct to say that there are 14 registers in the Z80, it's a bit misleading as well. Only one set of those registers is available for use at one time.

The Z80 has two types of instructions that allow access to the alternate registers: EX and EXX. The former exchanges the AF pair and the A′F′ pair, and the latter exchanges the other three pairs, (BC, DE, and HL for B′C′, D′E′, and H′L′), all at once. There are four other EX instructions that swap registers, but they operate only on the main register set.

The IN and OUT instructions are the last of the data-movement instructions. Some of those instructions operate only on a single byte of data, and others make it easy to move whole blocks of data. A simple I/O instruction would be:

IN A,n

The accumulator is symbolized by *A*, and *n* is a one-byte hex number specifying a particular port address. Since one byte is used to specify that address, the Z80 can address 256 different I/O ports.

When the Z80 executes an I/O instruction, several things happen. First, the port address specified in the I/O instruction is placed on the lower bits of the address bus (AO-A7). Second, the contents of the accumulator are put on the upper half of the address bus (A8-A15). Third, the $\overline{IORQ}$ line and the $\overline{RD}$ line go low. Finally, the data is transferred via the data bus to the accumulator. The whole process is quite similar to the way data is transferred to and from RAM (Random Access Memory). An OUT instruction would work in much the same way, but the $\overline{WR}$, rather than the $\overline{RD}$, line would go low.

DATA CHANGING INSTRUCTIONS

The second group of instruction covers many of the things we commonly do with hardware: arithmetic operations (ADD, SUB, CMP), that allow you to add, subtract and compare individual bytes, and logical operations (AND, OR, XOR), and bit operations (BIT, SET, RES, SHF, ROT) that allow you to examine and change individual bits.

If you've programmed in a high-level language like BASIC, the instructions in the third group should look familiar, since there are equivalents in all high-level languages. As mentioned above, the JUMP instruction is similar to BASIC's GOTO; CALL is similar to GOSUB, and RET is similar to RETURN.

The last group of instructions controls the operation of the Z80 itself, rather than directly manipulating or moving data. One very commonly used instruction is NOP, for NO OPERATION. It causes the Z80 simply to bide time for a full clock cycle. Among other things, programmers use NOP's to generate timing loops, and to reserve space in the middle of a program for code that will be added later.

The remaining instructions of that final group are all concerned with *interrupts* in one way or another. The Z80 allows three different types of interrupt, but they all operate in a similar manner. When a low is received on either of the Z80's two interrupt pins, normal program flow stops and, depending on how the Z80 is set up, program flow will continue at a special location in memory.

Unfortunately, to find out more about interrupts, software and other Z80 vitals, you're going to have to do some homework. We need some software to wake up our Z80 circuit, and we'll get into that. However, that software won't make much sense if you don't spend some time on your own reading about the Z80's instruction set.

So do some investigating, and don't be afraid to try burning an EPROM and telling our circuit to do something. Learning software design is very similar to learning hardware design—but with one big advantage:

It might not work, but it won't smoke or blow up!

Z80 DEMO PROGRAM

Now that we've built our Z80 system, the time has come, as they say in Transylvania, to bring it to life. When the circuit is powered up, the un-enlightened among your friends might get the impression that it's not doing anything. However, we in the know are perfectly well aware that it *is* doing something—it's waiting for us to tell it what to do. When it comes to microprocessors, there's one thing you should always remember: obedience and stupidity are twin virtues.

If you've done your homework and read up on the Z80's instruction set, and programming techniques in general, you may have come to the realization that our circuit is pretty limited. We've got a fair amount of program storage space in the EPROM, but RAM storage is limited to the Z80's internal registers, and our one-way I/O leaves a lot to be desired. So can we do anything with our circuit that is at all useful?

Let's take things one step at a time. First we'll write a short demo program to make sure the circuit is working. Then we'll talk about how we can expand the circuit to make it easier to accomplish something really useful. But before we start, I should mention that we're not going to go into the software in any great depth. If you're familiar with any kind of programming at all—even in the BASIC language—you shouldn't have any trouble following our discussion. Otherwise you *will* have trouble; so get out those data books and start reading!

Now for the demo program. Here, and throughout the rest of this column, all numbers will be in hex, unless otherwise specified. Now, since we've got a four-bit port, let's write a program that causes the Z80 to output values from 0 to F to that port.

SOFTWARE DESIGN

Writing software is simiar to designing hardware. The first thing to do is to get a clear idea of what you want to accomplish. With hardware you draw a block diagram;

with software you draw a flowchart, like the one shown in Fig. 8-3. The flowchart lets you see the way the program is going to operate without getting lost in a maze of low-level details. The flow of a small program like ours is more or less intuitive, but drawing flowcharts is a good habit to get into. Remember Grossblatt's Fourth Law: *You have to know the rules to break the rules.* In other words, don't look for shortcuts until you know where you're going.

Our flowchart is easy to understand. First we initialize things by loading appropriate values in the registers (which we'll think of as RAM). Then we send the number to be displayed to our latch. We wait for half a second, decrease the display number by one, and then do it all over again. That's repeated over and over until the displayed number is zero.

The actual program listing is shown in Listing 8-1, the Z80 instructions should be self-explanatory now that we understand the flowchart. The final version of the program added one thing not shown in the flowchart: a loop to repeat that whole process ten times and then quit. We use the H register to store the number we want to display, the L register to keep track of the number of times we've gone through the loop, and the DE register pair to keep track of the elapsed delay time.

The first instruction, XOR A, is a neat way to clear the accumulator using only one byte of program memory. What happens is that every bit in the register is XOR-ed with itself. We could get the same result by directly loading the accumulator with zero, but doing it that way takes two bytes.

The more bytes used, the longer the program gets, the more time it takes to run, and the more memory it uses. That's not important in our demo program, but another good habit to develop is that of saving memory, increasing speed, or both, as in the present case, by using "tricks" like that. Also, AND-ing, OR-ing, and XOR-ing a register with itself is useful for manipulating the Z80's flag bits with a single instruction. Any good book on programming the Z80 should be loaded with tricks like those. If they're not there, its not a good book. You might

Fig. 8-3.

Listing 8-1 Program.

Address	Op Code	Source Code	Comments
0000	AF	XOR A	Zero the Accumulator
0001	26 0F	LD H,0F	Set the display number
0003	2E 0A	LD L,0A	Set the loop counter
0005	7C	LD A,H	Load the Accumulator
0006	D3 FF	OUT (FF),A	Send it to the latch
0008	C3 00 11	JP 0011	Go to delay subroutine
000B	25	DEC H	Decrement port count
000C	2D	DEC L	Decrement loop counter
000D	C2 05 00	JP NZ 0005	Do again if not zero
0010	76	HALT	End of the program
0011	11 83 8B	LD DE,5161	Preset the delay loop
0014	B3	OR E	OR with the low byte
0016	1B	DEC DE	Decrement the counter
0015	7A	LD A,D	Transfer the high byte
0017	C2 14 00	JP NZ 0014	Jump back if not zero
001A	C3 0B 00	JP 000B	Return if finished

consider TAB's books #1656, *"The Programming Guide to the Z80 Chip"* by Phillip P. Robinson or #1491, "101 Projects for the Z80" by Frank P. Tedeschi and Robert Colon.

So, after initializing the registers, line 5 of the program sends the number to be displayed to the latch. If you're wondering why I'm using an OUT (FF), A instruction, the FF is the address of the port I want the number sent to. We could actually use any number because our circuit doesn't decode I/O ports, so any OUT instruction will wind up sending data to the latch. In a more complex system we'd have address-decoding circuitry that would select the proper port. In our circuit, the address lines are used only to load program instructions and data from the EPROM.

Our program now jumps to the delay loop that begins at line 11. We use the delay to slow down the program so you can see the countdown on LED's. Just connect them to the outputs of the latch with 330-ohm resistors. If you're really ambitious you could build a display circuit to have the output appear on a seven-segment readout.

Without the delay loop, the program would cycle so

quickly that you wouldn't be able to see any of the individual numbers. I used a full register pair to set up the delay time because the D and E registers together will allow any value up to FFFF.

Calculating the length of the delay isn't difficult. Each Z80 instruction takes one or more clock cycles, called *T* cycles, to execute. The number of cycles depends partly on the length of the instruction. Each trip through our delay loop takes 14 T cycles. Since we have a 1-MHz clock, or close to it, each cycle will take 1 microsecond for a total of 14 microseconds. If we want a delay of half a second we have to generate a loop that lasts half a million microseconds. Dividing 500,000 by 14 we get 35,714 or 8B83 hex.

Normally such a delay would be set up as a subroutine, callable by other routines in the program. But since we have no RAM, we can't do a subroutine call, because the Z80 automatically stores—in RAM—the address it is to return to after executing the subroutine. So we'll have to write our program without subroutines. We simply jump to and from the delay "subroutine" using JP, rather than using CALL and RET (GOSUB and RE-TURN, for you BASIC programmers).

ODDS AND ENDS

There are only two other things to talk about: the way instructions are printed and the way the program ends.

You probaly noticed that, in the Op Code column in Listing 8-1 the address and the data in line 11 appear to be written backwards. To avoid getting into a lot of messy details, you'll just have to accept the fact that that's the way it's done. The reason isn't really all that important—certainly it's not as important as remembering that it is done. Your reference book may give you the answer, but unlike programming tricks, if the answer isn't there, the book is not necessarily bad. Not all micprocessors use that low-high format, either; so be careful.

About ending the program: Since all it does is to count from fifteen down to zero, we could either have it go on forever or stop after a number of runs. Of course, we chose the latter, and the HALT instruction in line 10 ends the program. AFter the HALT executes, the only way to make the Z80 do anything useful is to reset it.

So, get an EPROM burned and plug it in. With some LED's connected to the latch you should see the count go from F down to 0 ten times. You'll get tired of watching if after a while, but it'll be thrilling the first couple of times—and at least you'll know your circuit works.

Now that we have a working circuit, what else can we do with it? By adding a couple of things, we can make that circuit one of the most useful we've ever put together—seriously! The first addition is a keyboard, and the second is RAM. I know it sounds as if we're talking about building a complete computer, but that's not the case at all.

A keyboard could be located in the regular memory address space; doing that would make getting data as simple as reading an address. A better way to do it would be to set the keyboard up at a port address as we did with our output latch. Of course, you would access the keyboard with an IN instruction as opposed to the OUT instruction we use in the demo.

Any serious use of that circuit will require getting data in and storing it somewhere. Using the registers for storage is fine for a demo, but for any serious use, we need some RAM.

The first thing we need to decide when adding RAM to the circuit is where it will be located. Since the Z80 starts program execution at power-up (or reset) from address 0000, it's a good idea to reserve low memory for ROM and high memory for RAM. A 2K EPROM might be addressed from 0000 to 07FF, and a 2K RAM might be addressed from F800 to FFFF. In order to access that additional memory, as well as the keyboard, you'd have to do more decoding of the $\overline{\text{RD}}$, $\overline{\text{WR}}$, $\overline{\text{MREQ}}$, and $\overline{\text{IORQ}}$ lines, but that's not the real problem. As you might have guessed, the real problem is, once again, software.

But let's forget about that for a moment; let's imagine some of the spiffy things you could do with the sort of circuit we've just described:

- Look up values in a table.
- Control peripheral devices.
- Test routines for the EPROM.
- Build an intelligent keyboard.

PUSHes, POP's, CALL's, and interrupts can't be used. Although the demonstration program avoids that problem by using JUMP's, an alternative would have been to stash calling addresses in one of the other Z80 register such as the IX or IY. Why not try that approach as it's a good exercise?

PROGRAMMING STYLE

The last comment I got in the mail was about the first line of the program, XOR A. Since the accumulator is loaded with a value in line 4 of the program, there's no real reason to zero it when the program starts.

Now I'm the first one to admit that the real hallmark of slick software is economy. Nobody gets more of a kick out of hacking bytes off a listing than I do. And when you deal in the real world where speed and memory constraints are very important considerations, an extra few bytes or so here and there can mean the difference between a working program and an embarrassment.

On the other hand, good programming skills (or skills of any sort), only come about by developing good habits, such as zeroing a register at the beginning of a routine, or preserving the environment before jumping to a subroutine. Unfortunately, habitual operations like those can't be applied blindly. Our XOR A doesn't hurt operation of the program, but it is unnecessary and can be deleted if you wish.

In our original discussion of the program, I stated Grossblatt's Fourth Law: You have to know the rules to break the rules. Let's put that another way: In the beginning you do it by the book, and when you think you know the book, you want to throw it out the window. But then again, it's probably better not to.

INDEX

INDEX

Other Bestsellers From TAB

☐ **EXPERIMENTS IN ARTIFICIAL NEURAL NETWORKS—Ed Rietman**

Build your own neural networking breadboards—systems that can store and retrieve information like the brain! This book shows you how to use threshold logic circuits and computer software programs to simulate the neural systems of the brain in information processing. The author describes artificial electronic neural networks and provides detailed schematics for the construction of six neural network circuits. The circuits are stand-alone and PC-interfaced units. 160 pp., 80 illus.

Paper $16.95   Hard $24.95
Book No. 3037

☐ **THE DIGITAL IC HANDBOOK—Michael S. Morley**

This book will make it easier for you to determine which digital ICs are currently available, how they work, and in what instances they will function most effectively. The author examines ICs from many major manufacturers and compares them not only by technology and key specification but by package and price. And, if you've ever been overwhelmed by the number of choices, this book will help you sort through the hundreds of circuits and evaluate your options—ensuring that you choose the right digital IC for your specific needs. 624 pp., 273 illus.

Hard $49.50   Book No. 3002

☐ **BUILD YOUR OWN 80286 IBM® COMPATIBLE AND SAVE A BUNDLE—Aubrey Pilgrim**

Assemble a powerful computer with all of today's dynamic options—at a fraction of the cost of a commercially made machine! Imagine building your own computer that has the ability to make use of the recently released OS/2 software! Much easier than you might believe possible, building your own 80286 machine requires no special experience. Pilgrim explains in detail how assembling your own high-quality 80286 can be economical, satisfying, and fun! 208 pp., 85 illus.

Paper $16.95   Hard $24.95
Book No. 3031

☐ **LEARNING ELECTRONICS: THEORY AND EXPERIMENTS WITH COMPUTER-AIDED INSTRUCTION FOR THE APPLE®—R. Jesse Phagan and Bill Spaulding**

Understand electronics with ease with the help of your Apple computer. This text is perfect for the beginning student or as a self-teaching guide for the hobbyist. It covers all the background theory necessary for a full understanding of electronics technology, and includes plenty of sample programs and hands-on laboratory exercises. BASIC computer programs for almost every chapter are in an exciting feature of this book. Quizzes and exams allow students to assess their progress.

Paper $16.95   Hard $24.95
Book No. 2982

Other Bestsellers From TAB